Expanding Your Sphere

Connecting With Strangers For More Realty Listings & Sales

Expanding Your Sphere

Connecting With Strangers For More Realty Listings & Sales

Steve Hoffacker

AICP, CAASH, CAPS, CGA, CGP, CMP, CSP, MCSP, MIRM

Expanding Your Sphere

Connecting With Strangers For More Realty Listings & Sales

Follow-Through® is a registered service mark of Hoffacker Associates. It relates specifically to customer contact strategies in real estate sales.

Realtor® is a registered service mark
of the National Association of Realtors.

Cover photo by Steve Hoffacker.

© 2013 by HOFFACKER ASSOCIATES LLC
West Palm Beach, Florida, USA

ISBN: 978-0-615-89686-1

———

To list and sell homes, you can wait for interested people to contact you from a variety of sources of marketing and promotion, or you can go out and attract them yourself. Rather than sitting back and waiting for people to contact you through conventional forms of advertising, promotion, and marketing — including the internet — a more intentional and reliable approach is to personally seek out, meet, contact, and begin developing relationships with people that might have an interest in working with you.

———

Other Sales Content
By Steve Hoffacker

To access or learn about books, eBooks, articles, blogs, commentary, videos, and other content by Steve Hoffacker for Realtors® and other real estate sales professionals, use the sites below.

"Hoffacker Associates" Website
stevehoffacker.com

Steve Hoffacker's Amazon.com Author Page
http://amazon.com/author/stevehoffacker

"Steve Hoffacker's Home Sales Insights" Blog
homesalesinsights.com

"Steve Hoffacker's Sales Quips" Blog
salesquips.com

"Steve Hoffacker's Success Quips" Blog
http://successquips.com

Steve Hoffacker and Hoffacker Associates can be found online at Facebook, Active Rain, Linked-In, Pinterest, Plaxo, YouTube, Twitter, Google+, Tumblr, and many other business, real estate, and social sites.

Table Of Contents

Preface

I appreciate that you bought this book and that you are reading it — particularly because of the importance of attracting new contacts from which you can make sales.

Because you thought enough of yourself to want to become an even better, stronger, more productive Realtor® or real estate professional than you are right now, you are reading this book.

It's also apparent that you are willing to take personal responsibility for generating the leads that it will take to sustain you in business.

You can take an active role and impact the amount of business you have through the contacts you generate.

This book is all about generating customers for yourself without relying on conventional advertising.

Typically, residential real estate is sold by having people interested in buying or selling contact you by visiting or calling your office or finding you online.

They may hear about you through traditional advertising, such as the newspaper or real estate magazines. They may also see your website or notice a billboard or other type of promotion. They might even find your card on a bulletin board or near the checkout at a store or restaurant.

Nevertheless, these are ways of attracting customers to you that are passive — they all require that someone else take the first step in creating the relationship.

Even social media is a passive type of lead generation because it first requires the connection with you before you can pursue it.

If you have ever wished that you could have more leads and more people interested in working with you to buy homes or list their existing ones, you can do that with the material that I am presenting ion this book.

Traditional advertising is fine, but you can supplement this and become much more of a factor in who you get to work with — particularly during slack times.

I don't want you to be dependant solely on the number of people that traditional and internet advertising produces for you. I want you to be a self-generator of sales leads and interested people.

Instead of complaining about the amount of responses you're getting (or not getting) from direct mail or traditional advertising, or asking your broker to run more ads to generate people for you to talk to, you now can do something about the amount of interested people you are adding to your database.

You can do this with no direct cost to you or your broker other than your typical telephone and postage usage — and some gasoline and an occasional cup of coffee.

In fact, I want you to act as though the only people that you're going to get to work with is that produced from your own efforts. Treat anything else you get from traditional advertising as a bonus.

I realize that this is probably a major paradigm shift for you, but I want you to act as if your entire income is going to come from sales and listings with people that you produce through your own efforts.

Now, I'm talking about direct efforts — not those from social media sites or other promotions that you run that are passive.

This book talks about identifying and working with people that you have not met previously — to introduce yourself to them and discuss what you can offer as you build a relationship with them.

Some will have an immediate need for your services, some likely will in the near future, and others will not be interested. However, many of them will point you in the direction of their circle of contacts and make the introductions for you.

This is the real value of working with strangers — having nearly a limitless pool of people to draw upon as well as

*the people that they know that otherwise would be
unavailable to you.*

*You supply the desire and the application. I'll supply the
words and strategies you can use to get you started.*

*Use them exactly as they are (or close to it), or use them
as a guide to develop your own style of contact.*

*It's time to take an active role in generating traffic for
yourself.*

Expanding Your Sphere

Connecting With Strangers For More Listings & Sales

1

Why Reach Out To Strangers?

Typical Advertising Is Passive

Many Realtors® and brokers think that the way to create interest in their listings is to advertise them in the newspaper, real estate or specialty magazine, or other places in print.

Recently, there has been a shift in this thinking, and print advertising has been largely replaced by advertising online or relying on the website to generate interest and sales leads.

Generally newspaper, magazine, and other print ads — and even online promotion or websites — go stale quickly, and may have you feeling that you don't have a lot of choice as to where to advertise — basically advertising where everyone else in your market is going.

Interested people may also learn about or contact you because they have seen a billboard.

You might even use radio or television advertising to attract attention and create new customers.

Regardless, this advertising, promotion, and marketing that is used to generate the majority of your sales leads and traffic is passive.

This doesn't make it bad. It just means that you can't control who will respond, how many people, what their needs or abilities will be, and how qualified or interested they will be to do business with you.

Why Typical Advertising Is Passive

The reason that conventional (sometimes called "traditional") marketing and advertising is passive is because you have no direct interaction with the people you are trying to reach until they decide to contact you.

For a passive message to work — print ad, radio or TV message, online ad, website, direct mail, or anything else that we typically use to get the word out — the person getting the message has to look at it or hear it. Then it has to register with them that they have a need and that this is a possible solution for them. Then, they have to initiate the contact by emailing you, visiting you in your office or at an open house, or calling you.

Referrals As Sources

Positive word-of-mouth (WOM), word-of-mouth-marketing (WOMM), and incidental referrals are very important — and an extremely economical way of attracting interested parties to see what you are offering.

You just can't depend on the frequency or quality.

Co-broking agents (from your own office or elsewhere) can be important sources of sales. Also, reaching out to those that you might want to work with is an important and valuable way to expand your business.

Generating Your Own Leads

If you are relying on the results of typical or traditional marketing to generate sufficient sales leads for your business — whether your company pays for the marketing, you pay for the marketing, or each of you does some of it — you are going to be disappointed at various times.

There are going to be slack times and periods when you seem to hit a streak of unqualified or unmotivated people to talk with about selling your existing listings or creating new listings.

Wouldn't it be nice to know that you have the ability to supplement the traffic that your company or traditional forms of marketing are supplying for you and to take responsibility for generating your own leads?

When newspaper advertising or other conventional ways of producing traffic or sales leads just aren't enough for you, when other brokers or agents aren't bringing enough people to you, when your website leads aren't as many as you would like, and even when your referrals — as great as they are to have — aren't coming at the pace you would like, you still have an option.

You can go after new leads and create them yourself. You can choose to be intentional.

Don't be content just with the people that walk through your front door, visit an open house or expo, call on the phone, or email for information.

You can go after and produce new leads by and for yourself.

Regardless of how many sales leads or traffic units you are getting from your traditional marketing efforts, you should never count on it. Be thankful for it, but consider it as a bonus.

Adopt the mindset that the only people you're going to get to make a presentation to and ultimately create a sale with are the ones you deliberately produce yourself.

Being Intentional

Being proactive or intentional is the opposite of waiting for people to come to you. It is taking the initiative. It is doing things on purpose.

Waiting in your office for people to come to you through conventional advertising and promotion is a typical response but insufficient to be successful.

This is passive marketing. You don't and can't know who they are until they take the first step and contact you. Then you can go from there.

On the other hand, proactive or intentional lead generation means empowering yourself to work with people you already know or to identify and utilize opportunities to meet people previously unknown to you (or at least people you hadn't met even if you did know who they were), introduce yourself, and begin a conversation.

By definition (at least the way I define it), intentional contact means meeting or talking with someone about what you are offering who has not reached out to you, may have minimal or no interest in the homes or properties you are offering, or may not ever contact or come to you on their own.

Intentional contact will open many doors for you.

It can lead people to you that you likely would never meet or talk to otherwise.

It's from this expanded circle or sphere of people — currently strangers to you — that you identify and meet that you can begin to generate leads and build sales.

You can also reach out to people that you already know and their circle of contacts, but this is the subject of a companion book called *"Utilizing Your Contacts: More Realty Listings & Sales With People You Already Know."*

Beginning With The Introduction

Intentional contact all starts with the *introduction*.

It means going out of your way — intentionally, proactively, and purposely — to meet someone you don't know and to introduce yourself to that person.

A proactive contact is not the time for a mini-presentation about what you are offering or listings you have available. Most of your discussion will come later — after you have met and talked initially.

In fact, you may not say anything about what you are offering other than the name of your company, the fact that you are a Realtor® or broker, and a general description of the type of properties or the market area and price range you focus on.

You may not have much more of a substantive discussion than just introducing yourselves to each other and exchanging business cards or getting their contact information.

This will open the door for a future conversation or connection.

The primary goal in an introduction is to secure contact information from the person you have met and get permission to contact them again.

What Comes Next?

After the initial introduction with someone, you can pursue an appointment to meet with them at their location, their home, your office, or a coffee shop.

You'll want to conduct a more thorough job of discovery about their interests in buying or selling (or both) — or who they know that might be looking for a new home.

Many of the people that you meet intentionally or proactively will not have a specific need for working with you when you contact them — or at least they may not initially. That's fine.

You are looking to develop leads — whether it's from the person you initially meet or someone that they in turn introduce you to. It's all part of the overall plan.

They may grow into a need for their first home or a new home over time or identify themselves as a candidate for a new home, but you also want to be introduced to people that they know who might have an interest in your listed homes and properties — or in working with you to market their existing homes.

And this is not just a one-time occurrence either. They can continue to lead you to new people over time.

This is the real value of intentional, proactive contact — being introduced or referred to other people whom you can approach.

This turns your efforts into a perpetual lead generating process.

The Concept Of Strangers

In this book, I specifically am talking about identifying and talking with people that you haven't met previously.

I want you to grow into a comfort level where you can begin approaching and talking to total strangers that might want to work with you or can lead you to people who will have an interest in your homes.

This will supplement the traffic you already get from traditional forms of advertising and promotion that your broker or company provides, and this will be in addition to the traffic that you can generate from working with people that you already know or have met — friends, relatives, associates, other Realtors®, and acquaintances.

Working with your existing circle or sphere of contacts is an important way of generating additional leads and referrals also. That's why I have created an entire book on it that forms a nice companion to this one (*"Utilizing Your Contacts: More Realty Listings & Sales With People You Already Know"*).

It's just that working with strangers gives you so much more latitude and flexibility in where and when you can see and meet people. You don't have to do anything special or go out of your way to meet them — unless you want to — because they are ever-present.

These aren't random strangers, but people that you meet during the course of your daily activities — at the gas station, the coffee shop, your office building, the market, the library, your kid's school, at lunch, at a seminar, or at the ballgame — anyplace there are people.

Beginning Where You Are

If you're not that comfortable approaching or talking to strangers — or you'd like to do it because you understand that it can help generate leads but aren't sure how it would be received — start with just a "hello" until it becomes more natural for you.

Also, don't put any pressure on yourself. There's no quota for how many leads you have to produce this way or how quickly you have to do it. Have fun with it.

You'll be surprised at how many times someone next to you in a store or at a public event will strike up a conversation with you. Just be open to it.

You will find that there are many people that you will want to meet, and it may take a little while or require a little extra effort to meet some of the people that you see on a regular basis because you don't normally speak to them.

You may have eye contact with them. You may exchange a smile. You may see them but aren't sure if they have ever seen you. You know them by site, but you've never been introduced to each other so technically they are a stranger.

Start the conversation, and see where it goes.

2

Being A Sales Lead Generator

Desiring More Traffic

I'm counting on you being the type of broker or Realtor® who is not content or satisfied with just waiting for the front door to open or the phone to ring to see which customer has found you through a newspaper ad, directional sign, website, internet, or other forms of advertising that your company provides for you or that you undertake yourself.

These conventional forms of lead generation are important, and there's absolutely nothing wrong with working with sales leads that are produced this way.

It's probably just not enough for you.

I'm sure you would like to talk with more people.

How often are there slack periods or lulls in the amount of people that you get to speak with in-person or interact with online or over the phone when you wish that you had more leads to work with or more people coming into your office or open house?

Maybe you'd like for your sales inquiries to be more consistent or that you could do something about the frequency of new contacts.

That's precisely why I have prepared this text for you.

You Can Make The Difference

You can be a catalyst for generating new sales leads and filling those void spots when contacts produced through other, more conventional sources are not as strong or consistent as you would like it.

You can make a difference — in fact, you can make *the* difference.

You can take the initiative to go outside the boundaries of your office to meet and talk to people who have a need for the type of opportunity you can provide or those who can lead you to people that you can help.

This is proactive, intentional contact, and it so often is the missing ingredient in being a totally productive real estate salesperson.

These are advanced techniques, but anyone can use them. It just takes the desire and the commitment to make it happen.

While we're focusing in this book on reaching out to strangers, working with people you already know is a valuable lead generation strategy also.

Both sets of people — those who are strangers and those you already know — are important for you to identify and work with to be more in control of your traffic production and sales output.

Taking Responsibility For Your Contacts

Rather than relying on the contacts that are produced though general advertising or even social media participation, you now can have a very real stake in the amount of people who visit or contact you and that you can talk with about your properties.

I have known Realtors® who have created such a following and referral base that they actually have decided not to take any floor time, walk-in, or non-"ask-for" sales leads.

The point is that you can create and generate a substantial portion of your contacts — even as much as all of it — through referrals and intentional, proactive self-generation of sales leads.

In this book, we specifically are talking about producing sales leads and contacts from total strangers and people you may know by sight but have never met.

Not A Mandatory Action

No one is forcing you to produce your own sales leads, but why not do all that you can to be successful?

Just think of the advantage that you'll have over other real estate professionals in your marketplace when you become responsible for producing your own sales leads and supplementing what you receive through traditional forms of marketing and advertising.

Remember that in this book we're talking about using a principle that few Realtors® ever employ — reaching out to strangers for potential sales leads.

This is even more beneficial than using people you already know to generate new business — while the number of people you know may be limited, the number of strangers that you can reach out and connect with is limitless.

The Power Of Being In Control

If you do nothing to change your method of lead generation, you'll be no different from any of the other Realtors® in your market.

You'll all be competing for the same limited number of potential buyers and sellers in your area that are reading the newspapers and real estate guides, searching the web, or driving your general area or neighborhood looking for signs identifying homes to visit.

However, you have the power to add substantially to the number of potentially interested people that you can talk to about listing their present home or finding a home to purchase — including both people that you already know as well as those who currently are unknown to you.

You can control the amount of sales leads that you have.

Be A Sales Leads Generator

If you want more potential business than you currently have, become a sales lead generator.

The added bonus to creating your own leads is that you don't need to share them with anyone.

This means greater customer loyalty and larger commission checks.

Knowing that you have the ability to generate your own leads to supplement what you get — or fail to get —

through more traditional means should be very empowering to you.

It can propel you into success while others in your marketplace are struggling or just working with the people that customarily contact them.

Instead of settling for just your share of available buyers in your marketplace that find you on their own through the efforts of conventional advertising and marketing, you can go way beyond that to identifying and producing your own leads and potential business.

You'll still get your share of contacts from conventional marketing, but you won't need to rely on it.

You'll be so much further ahead of your competitors and colleagues through your own efforts of lead generation that the potential business you receive though conventional advertising and marketing can just be considered a bonus.

3

Getting Started

Making A Conscious Decision

The first step in creating additional traffic for yourself
is deciding that you want to have more — and that
you'd like to personally do something about it.

Then you have to be willing to act.

Make the conscious decision that you would like to
begin generating additional traffic beyond what
appears through traditional advertising, signage, other
Realtors®, and incidental referrals.

This needs to be intentional and not just a wish or desire.

Then, you can go about accomplishing it.

You have so many resources available to you — ones
that perhaps you hadn't noticed or thought about until
now.

Two Approaches

You have two choices for identifying potential leads and expanding your opportunities for new business.

The first is going through people that you already know — regardless of how well — and the second is meeting and talking with people who until the moment you approach them are total strangers to you.

Then there is the spinoff that comes from both in terms of who they can refer and introduce to you.

This book deals specifically with the latter — meeting and talking with people that you don't already know.

My companion text focuses on working with people you already know and who know you.

Maybe some of the people that you think of as strangers are known to you already by sight but you've never actually met them or spoken with them. However, they might be people you're seeing and talking to for the first time.

Getting Started With Strangers

Constantly be aware of people around you and situations where you can meet people and talk with them about what you are doing.

Remember that the initial encounter with a stranger is just the introduction.

Don't attempt to go too far in the initial conversation — whether it's in-person, by phone, or through the mail.

You are not trying to make a sale (even though deep-down you might like to) on the initial contact.

You just want to open doors and pave the way for future conversations.

There Are People All Around You

There are many opportunities for you to find and meet people that you do not know: people you meet at the gas station, bank lobby, grocery store, convenience store, or home improvement store. Ditto for getting a coffee or going to lunch or dinner.

Add to that people selling their own homes, other brokers and Realtors® you know of but haven't met, other brokers and Realtors® you aren't aware of and obviously haven't met, business and professional people, contractors who work in your market area, people who call or email for information that you never meet in person, people who contact you that are shopping for someone else, and so many other situations — even people who approach you in public and ask for directions or talk about the weather or the previous day's game.

Remember that you are just trying to meet people and not make a presentation.

If you take mass transit or fly frequently, there are people sitting or standing next to you.

If you go to a professional sporting event or your child's ballgame, PTA meeting, or Scout meeting, there are people around you.

The point is that there are numerous opportunities throughout each day where you can meet and talk with people if you are aware of those opportunities and are prepared to utilize them.

The Point Of Your Initial Contact

Keep things in perspective.

When you call, meet, visit, or mail people that you have never met, you are not contacting them to try to get them to purchase a home from you or list their current one — unless it comes out in the conversation.

While ultimately you'd like for this to happen, initially you are just going for the introduction.

You have to meet people before you can develop a potential relationship with them and learn about their needs in selling their present home or getting another.

The reason you contact them intentionally is to make them aware of you and what you do — without delivering a strong request for their business.

It costs you absolutely nothing to approach a stranger, introduce yourself, and have a pleasant conversation with them — even if that's as far as it ever goes.

All you need to do is introduce yourself, mention what you do, find out who the other person is, and exchange business cards or contact information.

After you meet someone, you then can begin a dialog with them about what you're offering and learn if they might have a personal interest in buying or selling a home with you — or if they might know anyone who is interested in this.

You want them to lead you to their friends or acquaintances that are looking to buy a new home.

The Benefits Of Working With Strangers

Everyone travels in their own circle of friends and acquaintances. You might eventually find that you know some of the same people, but you are reaching out to strangers for three main reasons.

First, you can't rely just on people you already know or who come to you through normal advertising, the internet, other Realtors®, or incidental referrals.

You need to broaden your base, and you need to put a personal face on it.

You need to contact specific people, not just people in general that you're appealing to through advertising, promotion, and the internet.

Second, you want the people you are meeting — the people who have been strangers before you reached out to them but now are your new-found acquaintances — to lead you to people that they know who might be looking to buy or sell property.

Third, you are counting on creating an expanded network of visibility and word-of-mouth marketing about who you are and what you offer through the strangers you have met, their friends, and their expanded circle of family and contacts.

This potentially is a very large, almost limitless number of new leads and contacts.

Two Essentials To Have With You

Some of you may remember the old American Express ad that said *"Don't leave home without it"* — referring to their credit card. Even if you don't remember the ad, the message contains great advice for salespeople.

Make sure that you never leave your office or home — regardless of the weather or time of day — without a pen and a few business cards.

These are two extremely important business tools.

You never know when you may need either one, or both, to pursue your business.

When you meet someone that you want to talk to again, you must have the ability to contact them — and that requires their basic contact information.

If the person you meet doesn't have a business card, take the back of one of yours and have them write down their name and their preferred telephone number and email address on it — or do it yourself.

Either way, make sure you can read the information and that you know how to contact them again.

This is why most or all of the back of your card needs to remain blank and non-glossy so you can write on it.

People Like To Help

Later in this book, you will find formats, templates, and scenarios to use in planned and spontaneous face-to-face meetings with people, proactive telephone conversations, and outreach written contact.

You can use them word-for-word as they are, or you can use them as a guide and adapt them to your own personal style.

In reaching out to people — in this case strangers or people you have not formally met or spoken with previously — remember that people want to help you if they can. Tap into this trait and allow people to help you.

It's human nature to want to pitch in and help someone — to the extent of our resources, comfort level, and abilities.

Be Realistic About Your Outreach

Being proactive and generating your own traffic and contacts is a powerful way for you to have control over your business.

Just don't expect or count on this outreach to do more than it is capable of or designed to do.

It will not, in itself, make more sales or necessarily make the sales process any easier.

However, it will provide an opportunity for you to meet people and make an introduction that will produce new leads and contacts that can result in sales.

When you begin making the effort to meet people that

you have not talked to previously, two things will happen — you'll find people who are interested in working with you to sell their home or buy another, and you'll identify those who can lead you to people who are looking to do likewise.

As you approach people, you really shouldn't be interested in whether the conversation will focus on talking with them about their own needs or finding out about others they know — you benefit either way.

Regardless of what you discuss as you meet and connect with strangers, you'll have raised the level of awareness about what you are offering and made an intentional step toward attracting new leads.

Four Possible Outcomes

Whether you are meeting and talking with strangers or interacting with people that you already know, not everyone will have an immediate need for your services. Some might eventually, but that's only part of the total picture.

When you meet and approach strangers and introduce yourself to them, there are four possible outcomes — four things that can result.

First, they can refuse to talk with you or be disinterested in what you do. That's OK, shake it off and move on.

Second, they can have an immediate need to sell their current home and get another one, and they will want to engage you and start working with you.

Third, they may not have an immediate need to start looking for a new home, but they will in the future.

Fourth, they can introduce you or lead you to other people that they know whom they feel might have an interest in talking and working with you — with an immediate or future need.

This is the power of reaching out to strangers for their help.

Time To Get Started

Now, with a new understanding of how you want to use strangers to generate new leads and future sales, it's time to actually get started.

On the following pages, I present three consecutive chapters of scenarios for use in contacting people *in-person*, by *telephone*, and through the *mail*.

Add whatever techniques of your own that you like and feel free to use your own words and style, but this will get you started.

4

Meeting People Face-To-Face

The Benefits Of Meeting People

There are opportunities to meet people constantly. Many of the people that you see or meet are going to be total strangers to you at that moment. You don't know who they are — or if you do know them by sight or name, you have never spoken or been introduced.

As you shop, run errands, pick up the kids or attend events with them (if you have kids), buy gas, eat lunch, get a coffee, go to the store, go to the doctor or dentist, drop off and pick up your clothes at the cleaners, get your car serviced, live in your neighborhood, get your mail and packages, attend a block party, go to a PTA meeting, worship, eat dinner out, go places on your day off, go places with your spouse (if you're married), go biking or jogging, play golf, go to the pool or beach, visit the gym or spa, or serve on committees, you're are going to encounter people.

You likely do even more activities than this in a week's time — considerably more. The point is that there is never a shortage of people for you to meet.

It's learning to take advantage of these opportunities when you're around others to develop relationships and get their help in growing your business through the obvious networking possibilities that exist.

In some of your travels, you're going to see people that you already know or who are familiar to you by sight — even if you've never exchanged more than a glance, smile, wave, or "hello."

Most of the time, you'll likely see complete strangers. You may or may not even have eye contact with them.

Be open to the possibility of making introductions to total strangers, and then you can employ some of the contact strategies that I talk about in this book.

Expanding Your Network

Some of the scenarios presented in this chapter represent a deliberate, intentional action by you to reach out to people you don't know to identify those who have an interest in working with you or helping you.

For instance, contacts through business associations, apartment rental agents, lenders, people in large or expanding businesses, and people selling their own homes ("FSBO"s) are ones that you won't necessarily meet in your daily activities. You'll have to make a special point to reach out to them.

They have the potential of helping you by using your services themselves or making them available to their employees or members, referring people to you, letting you place your business cards in their establishment, allowing you to advertise on their website or newsletter, and helping you keep up with the news and happenings in your market area.

You have the potential of helping them by promoting them, using their products or services, and referring your customers to them.

After a relationship is established, there are several opportunities for additional interaction and mutual benefit from these people and companies that are strangers right now.

Adapting To Your Own Style

This chapter presents a sample of scenarios that you can use as you contact people in-person that you want to establish a dialog with — people such as those you have seen socially or at business functions but have never actually met or spoken with them, people that you are aware of but have never approached about helping you in your business, and others that you might happen to meet casually as you conduct your daily business.

In the scenarios and scripts that follow, there are many ways of saying the same thing — depending on your personal style and the degree of formality that might be called for at the time.

You can say *"I just stopped by to introduce myself,"* or you can express a similar meaning by saying that you *"dropped by,"* *"dropped in,"* or *"decided to visit."*

Instead of *"introduce myself,"* you could use *"say hello,"* *"meet you,"* or *"say hello and introduce myself."*

As for the people you are talking to or want to meet, you may not know whether it will be a man or a woman, so I have used *"he/she,"* *"his/hers"* or *"him/her"* in the scripts. Just choose the correct pronouns for the actual situation.

The same is true for people that you would like to have referred to you. They might be singles or couples, married or not. In many cases, I have just used the collective pronouns *"they,"* *"their,"* or *"them"* — both as a convenience and as the way that we generally talk in conversation. In actual usage, choose the correct pronouns for the situation.

Visit To Area Businesses

Use this scenario when you decide to visit a retail store, home improvement or décor center, furniture and accessories store, pharmacy, grocery, entertainment complex, arcade, donut shop, auto dealership, tire shop, boutique, equipment rental, hair salon, quick printer, service provider, or other businesses in your market to meet the owner, proprietor, or manager — to introduce yourself, and to open the door for referrals. You want to open a dialog, discuss how they can help you, determine who they know that has an interest in selling or buying a home — and you'd like to display your business cards or flyers for their patrons or possibly advertise with them in their establishment or on their website.

"Hello. Is <use their first name> in today (available)?"

[If you don't know the name of the person you should ask for, request the owner, proprietor, or manager.]

[You can mention that you belong to the same organization, that you attended the same event, that you are business neighbors, or that you would like their help for a minute. Add that they might not recognize your name or remember you.]

"I'm <your name>. I represent <name of your company

or branch office>."

"I wanted to meet him/her briefly and introduce myself. We are your neighbor at <street address, local landmark, or general area>."

NOT THERE — [The person you want is not present.] *"Do you know when he/she would have a minute for me to stop back and say hello (introduce myself)?"* [Agree on a day and time for the return visit.]

"Thanks for your time, and tell <person's name> that I'll stop by again on <day and time agreed on>. Good-bye."

NOW IS NOT A GOOD TIME — [You actually speak to the person you want, but they are unable to devote the time to you now.] *"I apologize for just dropping in like this."*

"I know that I didn't have an appointment and that this might not be a good (convenient) time for you. I'd really like to stop back by when you have a minute. I could use your help on something."

[Don't get into a discussion now of what you're looking for unless they decline to meet with you later.] *"When would it be convenient for me to come back?"*

[Wait for response. Agree on a day and time for the return visit or make the most of the situation while you're there.]

Agrees To Meet Again — *"Would you like me to come here, or would you let me buy you a cup of coffee?"*

[Wait for response about location of meeting and then confirm the location, day, and time.] *"I'll see you <specify the day> at <location>. Would you like for me to email you a reminder (confirmation)?"*

> **Yes** — *"Fine. I'll send you a note on <mention the specific day> to remind you of (confirm) our appointment on <day and time>."*
>
> *"Which email address should I use?"* [Obtain their preferred address and write it down.] *"See you then. Good-bye."*
>
> **No** — *"Fine. I'll plan on seeing you then <day, time, and place>. Good-bye."*

Declines To Meet Again — *"I understand how busy you must be. I apologize for just dropping in on you like this, but I wanted to meet you and introduce myself."*

"I really would like to talk to you for a minute. I can use your help." [Don't get into a discussion now of what you're looking for unless they decline to talk with you later.] *"Let me give you a call."* [Wait for response.]

> **Agrees to a call** — [Set a convenient day and time for you to call.] *"Thanks for your time. I'll call you*

<day and time agreed on>. Good-bye."

Does not agree to a call — *"I wanted to meet you and introduce myself so we'd each have a face to go with a name the next time we saw each other."*

"I dropped by not so much because I thought you might be looking for a new home — although you might be." [Let him or her tell you if they are in the market for a new home or look for body language that suggests they might be looking to sell their current home or get another one.]

"I thought that a person in your position might hear of or know two or three (one or two, a couple of) people who might be in the market for a different home that I should meet and talk with about how I can help them." [Wait for response.]

[If he or she volunteers a name or two, write it down and ask for a way to contact that person or persons. Be sure to note the correct spelling and pronunciation. Get first names so you don't sound like a telemarketer or solicitor when you call them, and get permission to use the person's name that is giving you the referrals when you contact the other people.]

They have names to give you — *"That's great. I will call them and learn what they are looking for (looking/wanting to do) and take it from there,* *and then I'll let you know what they had to say. Can you think of anyone else?"* [Wait for response.] *"Thanks for your help. Good-bye."*

No names to give you at this time — *"That's quite all right. If anyone does come to mind that you think I should talk to, please let me know."*

"In fact, let me give you some of my business cards in case you're talking to anyone that you think I should meet or talk to. If you can, let me who was interested enough to take my card or who you gave one to."

"Would it be OK if I left some of my business cards on your counter or if I came back with a small display?" [Wait for response, and accept the answer either way.]

"Thanks for your help. Good-bye."

IS AVAILABLE NOW — [The person you are calling on can actually talk with you now.] *"Great. I'll make this quick."*

"I just wanted to stop by to say hello and to introduce myself. I'd like to learn a little bit more about your business and let you know who we are. Also, I could use your help."

[Don't get into a discussion now of what you're looking

for unless they decline to meet with you later.] *"I'd like to set up a convenient time when we could meet for a few minutes either here or maybe you'd let me buy you a cup of coffee. Which one is better for you?"* [Wait for a response.]

[Agree on the location, and set a convenient time and day.] *"Thanks for your time, and I'll see you <place agreed on> on <day and time agreed on>. Would you like for me to email you a reminder (confirmation)?"* [Wait for response.]

Yes — *"Fine. I'll send you a note on <mention the specific day> to remind you of (confirm) our appointment on <mention the day and time>."*

"Which email address should I use?" [Write down their preferred address as you obtain it.] *"See you then. Good-bye."*

No — *"Fine. I'll plan on seeing you then <day, time, and place>. Good-bye."*

Visit To Area Professionals

Use this scenario when you decide to visit a physician, dentist, architect, consultant, appraiser, attorney, or other professionals in your market to meet the owner, principal, sole practitioner, consultant, or manager — to introduce yourself and also open the door for referrals.

You want to open a dialog, discuss how they can help you, determine who they know or have heard about that has an interest in selling or buying a home — and you'd like to display your business cards for their patrons.

———

"Hello. Is <use their first name> in today (available)?"

[The person you are asking for might greet you, or there might be a receptionist. Ask for the owner, principal, or manager. You can mention that you belong to the same organization, that you attended the same event, that you are business neighbors, or that you would like their help for a minute. Add that they might not recognize your name or remember you.]

"I'm <your name>. I represent <name of your company or office>. I wanted to stop by (meet) him/her briefly and introduce myself."

"We are your neighbor at <street address, local landmark, or general area>."

NOT THERE — [The person you want is not present.] *"Do you know when he/she would have a minute for me to stop back and say hello (introduce myself)?"* [Agree on a day and time for the return visit.]

"Thanks for your time, and tell <person's name> that I'll stop by again on <day and time agreed on>. Good-bye."

NOW IS NOT A GOOD TIME — [You actually speak to the person you want, but they are unable to devote the time to you now.] *"I apologize for just dropping in like this."*

"I know that I didn't have an appointment and that this might not be a good (convenient) time for you. I'd really like to stop back by when you have a minute. I could use your help on something."

[Don't get into a discussion now of what you're looking for unless they decline to meet with you later.] *"When would it be convenient for me to come back?"*

[Wait for response. Agree on a day and time for the return visit or make the most of the situation while you're there.]

Agrees To Meet Again — *"Would you like me to come here, or would you let me buy you a cup of coffee?"*

[Wait for response about location of meeting and then confirm the location, day, and time.] *"I'll see you <specify the day> at <location>. Would you like for me to email you a reminder (confirmation)?"*

Yes — *"Fine. I'll send you a note on <mention the specific day> to remind you of (confirm) our appointment on <day and time>."*

"Which email address should I use?" [Obtain the

preferred address and write it down.] *"See you then. Good-bye."*

No — *"Fine. I'll plan on seeing you then <day, time, and place>. Good-bye."*

Declines To Meet Again — *"I understand how busy you must be. I apologize for just dropping in on you like this, but I wanted to meet you and introduce myself."*

"I really would like to talk to you for a minute. I can use your help." [Don't get into a discussion now of what you're looking for unless they decline to talk with you later.] *"Let me give you a call."* [Wait for response.]

Agrees to a call — [Set a convenient day and time for you to call.] *"Thanks for your time. I'll call you <day and time agreed on>. Good-bye."*

Does not agree to a call — *"I wanted to meet you and introduce myself so we'd each have a face to go with a name the next time we saw or talked with each other."*

"I dropped by not so much because I thought you might need my services — although you might." [Let him or her tell you if they are in the market for a new home or look for body language that suggests they might be looking for a different home.]

"I thought that a person in your position might hear of or know two or three (one or two, a couple of) people who might be in the market for a different home that I could talk to or that should hear about how I might be able to help them." [Wait for response.]

[If he or she volunteers a name or two, write it down and ask for a way to contact that person or persons. Be sure to note the correct spelling and pronunciation. Get first names so you don't sound like a telemarketer or solicitor when you call them, and get permission to use the person's name that is giving you the referrals when you contact the other people.]

They have names to give you — *"That's great. I will call them and learn what they are looking for (looking/wanting to do) and take it from there, and then I'll let you know what they had to say."*

"Can you think of anyone else?" [Wait for response.] *"Thanks for your help. Good-bye."*

No names to give you at this time — *"That's quite all right. If anyone does come to mind that you think I should talk to, please let me know."*
"In fact, let me give you some of my business cards in case you're talking to anyone that you think I should meet or talk to. If you can, let me who was interested enough to take my card or who you gave one to."

"Would it be OK if I left some of my business cards on your counter or if I came back with a small display?" [Wait for response, and accept the answer either way.] *"Thanks for your help. Good-bye."*

IS AVAILABLE NOW — [The person you are calling on can actually talk with you now.] *"Great. I'll make this quick."*

"I just wanted to stop by to say hello and to introduce myself. I'd like to learn a little bit more about your business (what you do here) and let you know who we are. Also, I could use your help."

[Don't get into a discussion now of what you're looking for unless they decline to meet with you later.] *"I'd like to set up a convenient time when we could meet for a few minutes either here or maybe you'd let me buy you a cup of coffee. Which one is better for you?"* [Wait for a response.]

[Agree on the location, and set a convenient time and day.] *"Thanks for your time, and I'll see you <place agreed on> on <day and time agreed on>. Would you like for me to email you a reminder (confirmation)?"* [Wait for response.]

Yes — *"Fine. I'll send you a note on <mention the specific day> to remind you of (confirm) our appointment on <mention the day and time>."*

"Which email address should I use?" [Obtain their preferred address and write it down.] *"See you then. Good-bye."*

No — *"Fine. I'll plan on seeing you then <day, time, and place>. Good-bye."*

Visit To Area Business Organizations

Use this scenario when you decide to visit a business organization like the Chamber of Commerce, Business Development Board, or Convention and Tourism Bureau to meet the executive director, membership director, or key contact and introduce yourself. You want to meet and identify people who are interested in buying or selling a home due to transfers, promotions, relocations within the area, expansions, or new businesses coming into your area. Also, you want to become a member, get involved, advertise with them, learn about sponsorships, and display your cards in their office.

———

"Hello. Is <use their first name> in today (available)?" [If you don't know the name of the person you should ask for, request the executive director. If pressed for the nature of your visit, mention that you belong to their organization or would like to, that you want to introduce yourself, or that you would like their help for a minute.]

"I'm <your name>. I represent <name of your company or office>. I wanted to talk with <name of director> for just a minute and introduce myself."

NOT THERE — [The person you want is not present.] *"Do you know when he/she would have a minute for me to stop back and say hello (introduce myself)?"* [Agree on a day and time for the return visit.]

"Thanks for your time, and tell <person's name> that I'll stop by again on <day and time agreed on>. Good-bye."

NOW IS NOT A GOOD TIME — [You actually speak to the person you want, but they are unable to devote the time to you now.] *"I apologize for just dropping in like this."*

"I know that I didn't have an appointment and that this might not be a good (convenient) time for you. I'd really like to stop back or give you a call (sit down with you) when you have a minute. I could use your help on something."

[Don't get into a discussion now of what you're looking for unless they decline to meet with you.] *"When would it be convenient for you to talk with me?"*

[Wait for response. Agree on a day and time for the return visit or call — or make the most of the situation while you're there.]

Agrees To Meet Again — *"Would you like me to come here, or would you let me buy you a cup of coffee?"*

[Wait for their response about the location of the meeting and then confirm the location, day, and time agreed upon.] *"I'll see you <specify the day> at <location>. Would you like for me to email you a reminder (confirmation)?"*

   Yes — *"Fine. I'll send you a note on <mention the specific day> to remind you of (confirm) our appointment on <day and time>."*

   "Which email address should I use?" [Obtain their preferred address and write it down.] *"See you then. Good-bye."*

   No — *"Fine. I'll plan on seeing you then <day, time, and place>. Good-bye."*

Declines To Meet Again — *"I understand how busy you must be. I apologize for just dropping in on you like this, but I wanted to meet you and introduce myself."*
"I really would like to talk to you for a minute. I can use your help." [Don't get into a discussion now of what you're looking for unless they decline to talk with you later.] *"Let me give you a call."* [Wait for response.]

   Agrees to a call — [Set a convenient day and time

for you to call.] *"Thanks for your time. I'll call you <day and time agreed on>. Good-bye."*

Does not agree to a call — *"I wanted to meet you and introduce myself so we'd each have a face to go with a name the next time we saw each other."*

"I know that you must have Realtors® as members of your organization, but if you're not already referring people to a Realtor® or there is an opportunity for me to help, I'd like to talk with someone you know who might be selling their present home or looking for another one."

[Wait for response. See if there is an opportunity to work with this person and get referrals from him or her. You may need to join the organization.]

They Will Work With You — *"That's great. Are you aware of anyone right now who might be relocating to the area or is just in the market for a new home?"*

[Wait for response. If he or she volunteers a name or two, write it down and ask for a way to contact that person or persons. Be sure to note the correct spelling and pronunciation. Get first names so you don't sound like a telemarketer or solicitor when you call them, and get permission to use the person's name that is giving you the

referrals when you contact the other people.]

"I will call them and see what they are interested in doing, and then I'll let you know what they had to say. Thanks for your help. Good-bye."

They Already Have A Relationship — *"That's quite all right. I understand."*

[If they tell you that they will only send people to you through their existing Realtor® members, find out how you can become a member and get on their referral list.]

"Thanks for your time. Good-bye."

Is Available Now — [The person you are calling on can actually talk with you now.] *"Great. I'll make this quick."*

"I just wanted to stop by to say hello and to introduce myself. Also, I could use your help."

[Don't get into a discussion now of what you're looking for unless they decline to meet with you later.] *"I'd like to set up a convenient time when we could meet for a few minutes either here or maybe you'd let me buy you a cup of coffee. Which one is better for you?"* [Wait for a response.]

[Agree on the location, and set a convenient time and

day.] *"Thanks for your time, and I'll see you <place agreed on> on <day and time agreed on>. Would you like for me to email you a reminder (confirmation)?"* [Wait for response.]

> **Yes** — *"Fine. I'll send you a note on <mention the specific day> to remind you of (confirm) our appointment on <mention the day and time>."*
>
> *"Which email address should I use?"* [Obtain their preferred address and write it down.] *"See you then. Good-bye."*
>
> **No** — *"Fine. I'll plan on seeing you then <day, time, and place>. Good-bye."*

Visit To Expanding Area Businesses

Use this scenario when you decide to visit a local business that is expanding or hiring in your area — hospital, school board, local government, college or university, manufacturer, research and development, distribution, assembly, transportation, or other business — to meet the human resources director (HR), relocation specialist, or key contact and introduce yourself. Some of these organizations may already have relationships with Realtors®. If they do, try to establish yourself as well. You are interested in working with them as their employees are moving about in the area and new ones are coming into the area. Also, you're interested in possibly advertising with them, conducting seminars, or displaying your cards and flyers in their office.

————

"Hello. Is <use their first name> in today (available)?"

[If you don't know the name of the person you should ask for, request the HR director or relocation specialist. If pressed for the nature of your visit, mention that that you want to introduce yourself, or that you would like their help for a minute.]

"I'm <your name>. I represent <name of your company or office>. I wanted to talk with <name of director or specialist> for just a minute and introduce myself."

NOT THERE — [The person you want is not present.] *"Do you know when he/she would have a minute for me to stop back and say hello (introduce myself)?"* [Agree on a day and time for the return visit.]

"Thanks for your time, and tell <person's name> that I'll stop by again on <day and time agreed on>. Good-bye."

NOW IS NOT A GOOD TIME — [You actually speak to the person you want, but they are unable to devote the time to you now.] *"I apologize for just dropping in like this."*

"I know that I didn't have an appointment and that this might not be a good (convenient) time for you. I'd really like to stop back by when you have a minute (when it's convenient). I could use your help on something."

[Don't get into a discussion now of what you're looking for unless they decline to meet with you later.] *"When would it be convenient for me to come back?"*

[Wait for response. Agree on a day and time for the return visit or make the most of the situation while you're there.]

Agrees To Meet Again — *"Would you like me to come here, or would you let me buy you a cup of coffee?"*

[Wait for response about the location of the meeting and then confirm the location, day, and time.] *"I'll see you <specify the day> at <location>. Would you like for me to email you a reminder (confirmation)?"*

    Yes — *"Fine. I'll send you a note on <mention the specific day> to remind you of (confirm) our appointment on <day and time>."*

    "Which email address should I use?" [Obtain their preferred address and write it down.] *"See you then. Good-bye."*

    No — *"Fine. I'll plan on seeing you then <day, time,*

and place>. Good-bye."

Declines To Meet Again — *"I understand how busy you must be. I apologize for just dropping in on you like this, but I wanted to meet you and introduce myself."*

"I really would like to talk to you for a minute. I can use your help." [Don't get into a discussion now of what you're looking for unless they decline to talk with you later.] *"Let me give you a call."* [Wait for response.]

> **Agrees to a call** — [Set a convenient day and time for you to call.] *"Thanks for your time. I'll call you <day and time agreed on>. Good-bye."*

> **Does not agree to a call** — *"I wanted to meet you and introduce myself so we'd each have a face to go with a name the next time we saw or spoke to each other."*

"I know that you might already be working with some other Realtors®, but if there is an opportunity for me to help out with relocation or people looking for a new home in our area, I'd really like to do that — when you are bringing people into our area from out-of-town or you learn of someone here in the company during the normal course of your business who might be wanting a new (different) home."

[Wait for response. See if there is an opportunity to

work with this person and get referrals from them.]

They Will Work With You — *"That's great. Is there anyone right now who is relocating to this area, or are you aware of anyone in your organization who might be interested in getting a new home? I'd love to be able to talk with them."*

[Wait for response. If he or she volunteers a name or two, write it down and ask for a way to contact that person or persons. Be sure to note the correct spelling and pronunciation. Get first names so you don't sound like a telemarketer or solicitor when you call them, and get permission to use the person's name that is giving you the referrals when you contact the other people.]

"I will call them and see how I can help. Thanks for your time. Good-bye."

They Already Have A Relationship — *"That's quite all right. I understand. If there's any chance that I could help you or any of your employees in the future, I'd welcome the opportunity to talk with you or them."* [Wait for response.] *"Thanks for your time. Good-bye."*

IS AVAILABLE NOW — [The person you are calling on can actually talk with you now.] *"Great. I'll make this quick."*

"I just wanted to stop by to say hello and to introduce myself. Also, I could use your help."

[Don't get into a discussion now of what you're looking for unless they decline to meet with you later.] *"I'd like to set up a convenient time when we could meet for a few minutes either here or maybe you'd let me buy you a cup of coffee. Which one is better for you?"* [Wait for a response.]

[Agree on the location, and set a convenient time and day.] *"Thanks for your time, and I'll see you <place agreed on> on <day and time agreed on>. Would you like for me to email you a reminder (confirmation)?"* [Wait for response.]

Yes — *"Fine. I'll send you a note on <mention the specific day> to confirm (remind you of) our appointment on <mention the day and time>."*

"Which email address should I use? [Obtain their preferred address and write it down.] *See you then. Good-bye."*

No — *"Fine. I'll plan on seeing you then <day, time, and place>. Good-bye."*

Visit To New Area Businesses

Use this scenario when you decide to visit a local

business that is brand new to your market — to meet the owner, manager, human resources director (HR), relocation specialist, or key contact and introduce yourself. This is a startup company or one new to your market, and will vary in size and what they produce or offer at that location. Some of these organizations may already have relationships with Realtors®. If they do, try to establish yourself as well. You are interested in working with them as their employees are moving about in the area and new ones are coming into the area. Also, you're interested in possibly advertising with them, conducting seminars, or displaying your cards and flyers in their office.

_____

"Hello."

[You likely won't know the name of the person you should ask for unless you've done your homework ahead of time by calling to learn the name of the person you should speak with or determining it from their website. Otherwise, ask for the owner, manager, or HR director. If pressed for the nature of your visit, mention that that you want to introduce yourself and welcome them to the neighborhood.]

"I'm <your name>. I represent <name of your company>. I wanted to meet him/her and welcome you and your company to <name of your neighborhood, city, town, or area> (congratulate you on your new

business)."

NOT THERE — [The person you want is not present.] "*Do you know when he/she would have a minute for me to stop back and say hello (introduce myself, meet him/her)?*" [Agree on a day and time for the return visit.]

"*Thanks for your time, and tell <person's name> that I'll stop by again on <day and time agreed on>. Good luck here in < your city, town, or neighborhood>. Good-bye.*"

NOW IS NOT A GOOD TIME — [You actually speak to the person you want, but they are unable to devote the time to you now.] "*I apologize for just dropping in like this.*"

"*I know that I didn't have an appointment and that this might not be a good (convenient) time for you. I'd really like to stop back by when you have a minute (when it's convenient) so I could hear a little bit about what you do.*"

"*When would it be convenient for me to come back and meet with you?*"

[Wait for response. Agree on a day and time for the return visit or make the most of the situation while you're there.]

Agrees To Meet Again — *"Would you like me to come here, or would you let me buy you a cup of coffee?"* [Wait for response about the location of the meeting and then confirm the location, day, and time.] *"I'll see you <specify the day> at <location>. Would you like for me to email you a reminder (confirmation)?"*

> **Yes** — *"Fine. I'll send you a note on <mention the specific day> to remind you of (confirm) our appointment on <day and time>."*
>
> *"Which email address should I use?"* [Obtain their preferred address and write it down.] *"See you then. Good-bye."*
>
> **No** — *"Fine. I'll plan on seeing you then <day, time, and place>. Good-bye."*

Declines To Meet Again — *"I understand how busy you must be. I apologize for just dropping in on you like this, but I wanted to meet you and introduce myself — and welcome you to the (our) neighborhood (area)/ congratulate you on opening your new business."*

"Let me give you a call later. I'd like to hear more about what you do." [Wait for response.]

> **Agrees to a call** — [Set a convenient day and time for you to call.] *"Thanks for your time. I'll call you <day and time agreed on>. Good-bye."*

Does not agree to a call — *"I wanted to meet you and introduce myself so we'd each have a face to go with a name the next time we saw or spoke to each other."*

"I know that you might already be working with some other Realtors®, but if there is an opportunity for me to help out with relocation or people looking for a new home in our area, I'd really like to do that — when you are bringing people into our area from out-of-town or you learn of someone here in the company during the normal course of your business who might be wanting a new (different) home."

[Wait for response. See if there is an opportunity to work with this person and get referrals from them.]

They Will Work With You — *"That's great. Is there anyone right now who is relocating to this area, or are you aware of anyone in your organization who might be interested in getting a new home? I'd love to be able to talk with them."*

[Wait for response. If he or she volunteers a name or two, write it down and ask for a way to contact that person or persons. Be sure to note the correct spelling and pronunciation. Get first names so you don't sound like a telemarketer or solicitor when you call them, and get permission to use the person's name that is giving you the

referrals when you contact the other people.]

"I will call them and see how I can help. Thanks for your time. Good-bye."

They Already Have A Relationship — *"That's quite all right. I understand. If there's any chance that I could help you or any of your employees in the future, I'd welcome the opportunity to talk with you or them."* [Wait for response.] *"Thanks for your time. Good-bye."*

Is Available Now — [The person you are calling on can actually talk with you now.] *"Great. I'll make this quick."*

"I just wanted to stop by to say hello and to introduce myself. Also, I could use your help."

[Don't get into a discussion now of what you're looking for unless they decline to meet with you later.] *"I'd like to set up a convenient time when we could meet for a few minutes either here or maybe you'd let me buy you a cup of coffee. Which one is better for you?"* [Wait for a response.]

[Agree on the location, and set a convenient time and day.] *"Thanks for your time, and I'll see you <place agreed on> on <day and time agreed on>. Would you like for me to email you a reminder (confirmation)?"*

[Wait for response.]

Yes — *"Fine. I'll send you a note on <mention the specific day> to confirm (remind you of) our appointment on <mention the day and time>."*

"Which email address should I use? [Obtain their preferred address and write it down.] See you then. Good-bye."

No — *"Fine. I'll plan on seeing you then <day, time, and place>. Good-bye."*

Strategic Visit To Other Realty Offices

Use this scenario when you decide to visit a particular realty office in your marketplace to meet the manager or broker and introduce yourself. You are interested in having them as a professional colleague, a strategic resource, and to help you sell your listings.

———

"Hello. Is <use their first name> in today (available)?" [The broker's name will be on the door if you need it.]

"I'm <your name>, a fellow Realtor®. I represent <name of your company or office>. I wanted to introduce myself to <broker>."

"We are your neighbor at <street address, local

landmark, or other description that they would recognize>."

NOT THERE — [The person you want to see is not present.] *"Do you know when he/she would have a minute (be available) for me to stop back (drop in) and say hello (introduce myself)?"* [Agree on a day and time for the return visit.]

"Thanks for your time, and tell <person's name> that I'll stop by again on <day and time agreed on>. Good-bye."

NOW IS NOT A GOOD TIME — [You actually speak to the person you want, but they are unable to devote the time to you now.] *"I apologize for just dropping in like this. I just wanted to meet you and introduce myself."*

"I'm sorry I caught you at an inconvenient (busy) time, but I want to discuss a mutually beneficial business relationship with you and I'd really like to stop back by when you have a minute."

[Don't get into a discussion now of what you're looking for unless they decline to meet with you later.] *"When would it be convenient for me to come back (stop in again, return)?"*

[Wait for response. Agree on a day and time for the return visit or make the most of the situation while you're there.]

Agrees To Meet Again — *"Would you like me to come here, or would you let me buy you a cup of coffee?"*

[Wait for response about location of meeting and then confirm the location, day, and time.] *"I'll see you <specify the day> at <location>. Would you like for me to email you a reminder (confirmation)?"*

> **Yes** — *"Fine. I'll send you a note on <mention the specific day> to remind you of (confirm) our appointment on <day and time>."*
>
> *"Which email address should I use?"* [Obtain their preferred address and write it down.] *"See you then. Good-bye."*
>
> **No** — *"Fine. I'll plan on seeing you then <day, time, and place>. Good-bye."*

Declines To Meet Again — *"I understand how busy you must be. I apologize for just dropping in on you like this, but I wanted to meet you and introduce myself and take it from there."*

"I really would like to talk to you for a minute. I can use your help." [Don't get into a discussion now of what you're looking for unless they decline to talk with you later.] *"Let me give you a call."* [Wait for response.]

Agrees to a call — [Set a convenient day and time for you to call.] *"Thanks for your time. I'll call you <day and time agreed on>. Good-bye."*

Does not agree to a call — *"I wanted to meet you and introduce myself so we'd each have a face to go with a name the next time we saw or spoke to each other."*

"I dropped by to talk about how we might establish a mutually beneficial business relationship." [If there seems to be some interest in what you're suggesting or mentioning, set an appointment to meet or talk more later. If there does not seem to be any interest in working with you or even hearing about your proposal, conclude your conversation and leave.] *"Good-bye."*

IS AVAILABLE NOW — [The person you are calling on can actually talk with you now.] *"Great. I'll make this quick."*

"I just wanted to stop by to say hello and to introduce myself. Also, I could use your help."

[Don't get into a discussion now of what you're looking for unless they decline to meet with you later.] *"I'd like to set up a convenient time when we could meet for a few minutes either here or maybe you'd let me buy you a cup of coffee. Which one is better for you?"*

[Wait for a response.]

[Agree on the location, and set a convenient time and day.] *"Thanks for your time, and I'll see you <place agreed on> on <day and time agreed on>. Would you like for me to email you a reminder?"* [Wait for response.]

Yes — *"Fine. I'll send you a note on <mention the specific day> to remind you of our appointment on <mention the day and time>."*

"Which email address should I use?" [Obtain their preferred address and write it down.] *"See you then. Good-bye."*

No — *"Fine. I'll plan on seeing you then <day, time, and place>. Good-bye."*

Meeting New People

Use this scenario when you meet someone for the first time in public or socially — either planned or spontaneous — to introduce yourself and sustain the conversation. This could be at the gas pump, convenience store, your child's school, PTA meeting, your child's Scout meeting or athletic event, a neighborhood block party, a sporting event, a festival, a store or retail establishment, standing in line, a restaurant or coffee shop, a bar, a seminar, mixer, party, class, services provided at your home, driving through your market area, or anywhere someone might be that you could have a chance meeting. After the introduction, you can identify people who are interested in buying a new home or know people that are.

———

"Hi. I'm <your name>." [Learn their name and the correct pronunciation.] *"I'm pleased to meet you."*

[When the discussion gets around to what each of you does, exchange business cards or give them your card and make a note of their contact information.]

[Make a brief statement about what you primarily focus on — first-time buyers, vacation properties, waterfront, luxury homes, condominiums, foreclosures, short sales, farms, investment property — and where your office is located.]

"I really would like to talk to you a little more about what we do and what your present or future needs might be. May I give you a call?" [Wait for response, and be prepared for either a "yes" or "no" answer.]

Agrees To A Call — [Set a time and date or an approximate time frame for the call.] *"Nice meeting you and I'll call you <day and time agreed on> (in a couple of days). Good-bye."*

Does Not Agree To A Call — *"I'm glad to have met you, and I'd like to know if you think you might be interested in selling your present home or purchasing another in the foreseeable future — or if you know (can think of) one or two people (anyone) who might be looking for a new home."*

[Let them tell you if they are in the market for a new home or look for body language that suggests they might be looking for a new home themselves. If they volunteer a name or two, write it down and ask for a way to contact that person or persons. Be sure to note the correct spelling and pronunciation. Get first names so you don't sound like a telemarketer or solicitor, and get permission to use the person's name that is giving you the referrals when you contact the other people.]

They have names to give you — *"That's great. I will call them and see how I can help them. Can you think of anyone else?"* [Wait for response.] *"Thanks for your help. Good-bye."*

No names to give you at this time — *"That's quite all right. If anyone does come to mind that you think I should talk with. please let me know."*

"In fact, let me give you some of my business cards in case you're talking to anyone that you think I should meet or talk to. I'll check with you in a couple of weeks to see if anyone has come to

mind. Thanks for your help. Good-bye. "

Visit With A "FSBO"

Use this scenario when you decide to knock on
someone's door in your market or farm area that has a
"For Sale By Owner" or similar sign in their yard.
Assure them that you are not trying to sell their home
for them although you really would like to get the
listing on it. Be mindful that they may have had several
other Realtors® already contact them and might be
defensive or annoyed because of this. You want to
meet them because this is your market area, you are
curious about the interest they've had in their home,
you want to talk with them about a new home if they
haven't selected it already, and you want to know who
else they know who might be interested in looking for a
new home.

———

*"Hello. I'm <you name> from <name of your company
or office>."* [Hand them your business card, and learn
their name.]

*"I saw your sign, and I think it's great that you are
trying to sell your home by yourself.* **I didn't come by
to talk to you about helping you to sell your home.**"
[Make a sincere and emphatic point about this.] *"It's
just that this is my market area that I drive through
regularly — that's why I noticed your sign."*

"I just wanted to meet you and find out if you've made any plans for your next home after you sell this one." [Wait for response, and be prepared for either a "yes" or "no" answer.]

No Plans For Next Home — *"I'd love to talk with you (learn what you might be looking for) when you've got a few minutes."* [Set a convenient time for you to talk again and agree to it.]

"Would you like for me to stop back by or give you a call — or maybe you'd let me buy you a cup of coffee?" [Wait for response.]

"Nice meeting you and I'll call you (stop back) <day and time agreed on>." [Confirm their telephone number from the yard sign if you have agreed to call them.] *"Good-bye."*

Already Decided On Next Home — [Congratulate them on the selection of their next home and ask them a little about it, why they selected it, and how they learned about it.] *"Do you know anyone else who might be in the market for a new home that I could talk to? I might be able to help them."*

[Wait for response. If he or she volunteers a name or two, write it down and ask for a way to contact that person or persons. Be sure to note the correct spelling and pronunciation. Get first names so you don't sound like a telemarketer or solicitor when you call them, and get permission to use the person's name that is giving you the referrals when you contact the other people.]

They have names to give you — *"That's great. I will call them and see how I can help them. Can you think of anyone else?"* [Wait for response.]

"Thanks for your help. Good-bye."

No names to give you at this time — *"That's quite all right. If anyone does come to mind that you think should I should talk to, please let me know. I would be happy to give them a call."*

"In fact, let me give you some of my business cards in case you're talking to anyone that you think I should meet or talk to. May I check with you in a couple of weeks to see if anyone has come to mind?" [Wait for response.]

"Thanks for your help. Good-bye."

Visit To An "Open House"

Use this scenario when you decide to visit an advertised "open house," or one in your market area that you find with a directional sign — to meet the Realtor® hosting it and introduce yourself and your company. Assure them that you didn't come to interfere or walk off with any of their customers. You just want to meet them and look at the property to familiarize yourself with it. You may be able to form a strategic alliance this way or find a property to show to your customers.

———

"Hello. I'm <you name> from <name of your company or office>." [Hand them your business card, and learn their name. Get their card, too.]

"I saw your sign, and I wanted to stop by and meet you. This is my market area (This is my market area, too) — that's why I noticed your sign. I thought this would be a good opportunity to say "hello" and meet you since you are active (have a listing) in this area."

[If you recognize their name from their signs in your market area, try to get them as a strategic partner to show each other's listings for potential co-broke sales. If their name is not familiar to you or they tell you that this is not their market area but just a listing they obtained, offer your help as the expert in the area and discuss helping them to make the sale,]

"I dropped by to talk about how we might establish a mutually beneficial business relationship." [If there seems to be some interest in what you're suggesting or mentioning, set an appointment to meet or talk more

later. If there does not seem to be any interest in working with you to help sell this home or even hearing about your proposal, conclude your conversation and leave.] *"Good-bye and good luck with your open house."*

[Agree on the location, and set a convenient time and day.] *"Thanks for your time, and I'll see you <place agreed on> on <day and time agreed on>. Would you like for me to email you a reminder?"* [Wait for response.]

> **Yes** — *"Fine. I'll send you a note on <mention the specific day> to remind you of our appointment on <mention the day and time>."*

> *"Which email address should I use?"* [Obtain their preferred address and write it down.] *"See you then. Good-bye and good luck with your open house."*

> **No** — *"Fine. I'll plan on seeing you then <day, time, and place>. Good-bye and good luck with your open house."*

Visit To Shows, Fair, And Expos

Use this scenario when you decide to visit or attend a trade show, home show, boat show, convention, conference, agricultural fair, or other type of expo or show — open to the public or not — to meet people and begin cultivating relationships that you can use later. Just go for the introductions and learning a little bit about the people you meet. They can be exhibitors, presenters, or attendees, and the events can be at held at hotels, expo or convention centers, arenas, armories, stadiums, fairgrounds, or other venues.

———

[When you walk up and meet someone staffing the booth or display] *"Hello. I'm <your name>."*

[Because of the nature of a trade show or expo, people are exhibiting so that they can meet and contact as many people as possible about their products and services. Take full advantage of it. Be sure to show some interest in what they are offering. If you're not familiar with it, ask questions. If you could possibly purchase what they offer or use it to enhance the homes you sell, ask questions from that standpoint. Engage in small talk as well — depending on whether they can devote time to talking with you or they need to talk with other people. They likely will have business cards on the table. If not, it's simple enough to ask for one. This is an ideal setting for meeting people that you can talk to again after the event.]

[Primarily go for the introduction, but depending on how much time you have for conversation, you might be able to begin a discussion about what you do or begin determining their needs. There usually is a lot of opportunity for give-and-take in these type of situations. Take advantage of it.]

[The exhibitor you're meeting may call you after the event, but you can telephone him or her as well because your agendas are different. Your want to talk with them about selling their home or helping them find another one, or you want them to give you referrals. They want you to purchase what they offer.]

[You don't have to pretend that you're interested in their product or service if you're not. On the other hand, if you are, that's fine. Either way, transition into talking about what you want on the post-event phone call.]

[As far as attendees at the event that you happen to meet, treat them the same as people you meet at a chance encounter, outlined on pages 80-82. Go primarily for the introduction. If more conversation ensues, fine. However, stop short of setting an appointment for anything other than a phone call. You don't want it to seem that you're just collecting business cards or that you are acting like an exhibitor.]

[Make sure you have something to write down their contact information. You may want to skip handing your business card and just email them your contact information to keep it softer and give you another reason to reach out to them after the event.]

Visit To Apartment Rental Agents

Use this scenario when you decide to visit an apartment rental office in your marketplace to meet the manager, resident broker, or leasing agent — to introduce yourself and discuss how you can help their tenants when they are ready for home ownership and how they can help you when you need short-term housing for your customers when they must move out of their current home or relocate to your area before they can close on the home they're getting with you. Also, you're interested in possibly advertising with them, conducting seminars, or displaying your cards and flyers in their office. You also can learn about prevailing rents to use in making a case for homeownership with your buyers.

———

"Hello. Is <use their first name> in today (available)?"

[If you don't know the name of the person you should ask for, request the manager, broker, or leasing agent.]

"I'm <your name> from <name of your company or office>. I wanted to talk with <name of manager, broker, or agent> for just a minute and introduce myself."

NOT THERE — [The person you want to talk with is not

present.] *"Do you know when he/she would have a minute (be available) for me to stop back and say hello (introduce myself)?"* [Agree on a day and time for the return visit.]

"Thanks for your time, and tell <person's name> that I'll stop by again on <day and time agreed on>. Good-bye."

NOW IS NOT A GOOD TIME — [You actually speak to the person you are calling on, but they are unable to devote the time to you now.] *"I apologize for just dropping in like this. I just wanted to meet you and introduce myself."*

"I'm sorry I caught you at an inconvenient (busy) time, but I want to discuss a mutually beneficial business relationship with you and I'd really like to stop back by when you have a minute."

[Don't get into a discussion now of what you're looking for unless they decline to meet with you later.] *"When would it be convenient for me to come back (stop in again)?"*

[Wait for response. Agree on a day and time for the return visit or make the most of the situation while you're there.]

Agrees To Meet Again — *"Would you like me to come*

here, or would you let me buy you a cup of coffee?"

[Wait for response about location of meeting and then confirm the location, day, and time.] *"I'll see you <specify the day> at <location>. Would you like for me to email you a reminder (confirmation)?"*

> **Yes** — *"Fine. I'll send you a note on <mention the specific day> to remind you of (confirm) our appointment on <day and time>."*
>
> *"Which email address should I use?"* [Obtain their preferred address and write it down.] *"See you then. Good-bye."*
>
> **No** — *"Fine. I'll plan on seeing you then <day, time, and place>. Good-bye."*

Declines To Meet Again — *"I understand how busy you must be. I apologize for just dropping in on you like this, but I wanted to meet you and introduce myself."*

"I really would like to talk to you for a minute. I can use your help." [Don't get into a discussion now of what you're looking for unless they decline to talk with you later.] *"Let me give you a call."* [Wait for response.]

> **Agrees to a call** — [Set a convenient day and time for you to call.] *"Thanks for your time. I'll call you <day and time agreed on>. Good-bye."*

Does not agree to a call — *"I wanted to meet you and introduce myself so we'd each have a face to go with a name the next time we saw each other."*

"I dropped by to talk about how we might establish a mutually beneficial business relationship." [If there seems to be interest in what you're discussing, pursue setting an appointment to meet or talk more later. If there does not seem to be any interest, conclude your conversation and leave.] *"Good-bye."*

Is AVAILABLE NOW — [The person you are calling on can actually talk with you now.] *"Great. I'll make this quick."*

"I'd like to set up a time to meet with you for a few minutes and discuss creating a mutually beneficial business relationship."

[Don't get into a discussion now of what you're looking for or have in mind unless they decline to meet with you later.] *"We can meet here, or you could let me buy you a cup of coffee. Which one is better for you?"* [Wait for a response.]

[Agree on the location, and set a convenient time and day.]

"Thanks for your time, and I'll see you <place agreed on> on <day and time agreed on>. Would you like for me to email you a reminder (confirmation)?" [Wait for

response.]

Yes — *"Fine. I'll send you a note on <mention the specific day> to remind you of (confirm) our appointment on <mention the day and time>."*

"Which email address should I use? [Obtain their preferred address and write it down.] *"See you then. Good-bye."*

No — *"Fine. I'll plan on seeing you then <day, time, and place>. Good-bye."*

Visit To Lenders And Mortgage Brokers

Use this scenario when you decide to visit a lender, bank, or a mortgage broker at their office in your marketplace to meet the manager, loan officer, or mortgage broker — to introduce yourself and discuss opportunities for you to work with people that have come to them to pre-qualify for financing without having a particular new home selected in advance — as well as other people they may know or be aware of who are looking to list their current home or purchase a new one. You also want to explore the types of loans they can make to your customers and identify some preferred lenders.

———

"Hello. Is <use their first name> in today (available)?"

[If you don't know the name of the person you should ask for, request the manager, broker, or loan officer.]

"I'm <your name>. I represent <name of your company or office>. I wanted to meet <name of manger, mortgage broker, or loan officer> and introduce myself and our company."

NOT THERE — [The person you want to talk with is not present.] *"Do you know when he/she would have a minute for me to stop back and introduce myself?"* [Agree on a day and time for the return visit.]

"Thanks for your time, and tell <person's name> that I'll stop by again on <day and time agreed on>. Good-bye."

NOW IS NOT A GOOD TIME — [You actually speak to the person you want to talk with, but they are unable to devote the time to you now.] *"I apologize for just dropping in like this. I wasn't sure if you'd have time for me now, but I wanted to meet you and introduce myself."*

"I'm sorry I caught you at an inconvenient (busy) time, but I want to discuss a mutually beneficial business relationship with you and I'd really like to stop back by and talk with you for a few minutes when it's convenient."

[Don't get into a discussion now of what you're looking

for unless they decline to meet with you later.] *"When would it be convenient (good) for me to come back?"*

[Wait for response. Agree on a day and time for the return visit or make the most of the situation while you're there.]

Agrees To Meet Again — *"Would you like me to come here, or would you let me buy you a cup of coffee?"*

[Wait for their response about the location of the meeting and then confirm the location, day, and time.] *"I'll see you <specify the day and time> at <location>. Would you like for me to email you a reminder (confirmation)?"*

> **Yes** — *"Fine. I'll send you a note on <mention the specific day> to remind you of (confirm) our appointment on <day and time>. Which email address should I use?"* [Obtain their preferred address and write it down.] *"See you then. Good-bye."*

> **No** — *"Fine. I'll plan on seeing you then <day, time, and place>. Good-bye."*

Declines To Meet Again — *"I understand how busy you must be. I apologize for just dropping in on you like this, but I wanted to meet you and introduce myself."*

"I really would like to talk to you for a minute. I can

use your help." [Don't get into a discussion now of what you're looking for unless they decline to talk with you later.] *"Let me give you a call."* [Wait for response.]

Agrees to a call — [Set a convenient day and time for you to call.] *"Thanks for your time. I'll call you <day and time agreed on>. Good-bye."*

Does not agree to a call — *"I stopped by because I wanted to meet you and introduce myself so we'd each have a face to go with a name the next time we saw or spoke with each other."*

"I want to talk about how we might establish a mutually beneficial business relationship." [If there seems to be interest in what you're discussing, pursue setting an appointment to meet or talk more later. If there does not seem to be any interest, conclude your conversation and leave.] *"Good-bye."*

Is Available Now — [The person you are calling on can actually talk with you now.] *"Great. I'll make this quick."*

"I just wanted to stop by for a minute to meet you and introduce myself. I would like to talk with some more when it's convenient about creating a mutually beneficial business relationship."

[Don't get into a discussion now of what you're looking

for unless they decline to meet with you later and you need to go ahead and present your case.] *"We can meet here, or you could let me buy you a cup of coffee. Which one is better for you?"* [Wait for a response.]

[Agree on the location, and set a convenient time and day.]

"Thanks for your time, and I'll see you again at <place agreed on> on <day and time agreed on>."

"Would you like for me to email you a reminder (confirmation)?" [Wait for response.]

> **Yes** — *"Fine. I'll send you a note on <mention the specific day> to remind you of (confirm) our appointment on <mention the day and time>."*
>
> *"Which email address should I use?"* [Obtain their preferred address and write it down.] *"See you then. Good-bye."*
>
> **No** — *"Fine. I'll plan on seeing you then <day, time, and place>. Good-bye."*

5

Connecting By Telephone

The Value Of Telephone Contact

In addition to using personal introductions and interaction to reach out and meet people, the telephone provides many of the same opportunities without needing to be face-to-face with someone.

In many cases, it's even better than face-to-face encounters because you might be working with a lead provided by someone else, or you might be contacting someone that is difficult to reach in-person.

By attempting to reach out and create a relationship with someone whom you haven't met, it's trickier than approaching people you already know. You can't just open up your Rolodex, database, or smartphone, and begin calling people.

Still, you may have identified the names and phone numbers for brokers, appraisers, contractors, mortgage brokers, lenders, home inspectors, designers, interior decorators, architects, home stagers, leasing agents, suppliers, tradespeople, businesses, and services in your area that you want to contact.

That's the first step. Assemble a list of names and phone numbers of people or businesses that you want to contact. In some cases, you'll only know the business name and not the name of the actual person you need to contact.

Continuously add to this list as you see billboards and company vehicles, read news articles, see realty yard signs and those by FSBOs, connect with people on social media, and identify other sources of names for you to contact.

Constantly be open to new sources of leads.

Telephoning Can Be Efficient

You need to meet and talk with people who can help you. You're not always in a position where you can drive to their location, and letters can takes days to arrive. Emails aren't appropriate for an introduction.

Other than meeting someone face-to-face when that is convenient, telephone contact is the next most efficient method to use.

Face-to-face contact isn't always possible due to travel distances and the schedules of people you want to meet with and talk to in-person, so telephone contact can actually be a more efficient use of your time to establish the initial contact and determine the next course of action.

Expanding Your Comfort Zone

This chapter focuses specifically on using the telephone (it doesn't matter whether it's a cell phone or landline) as a proactive, intentional means of contact to reach out and connect with people that are strangers to you at the moment you are calling them.

They are strangers because you have never spoken with them before or had any contact with them other than possibly seeing them at a meeting without speaking to them or having connected with them on social media without developing that contact.

This may not be comfortable for you immediately, and you may have to grow into a comfort level.

There are parts of this strategy that just might be beyond what you're willing to do to right now. That's OK.

Proactive, intentional telephone contact is a very

effective tool to use. If you're not ready for it now, it'll be available when you do decide to use it.

Using The Telephone Effectively

For those of you who are comfortable picking up the phone and reaching out to people you've never met or talked to before, I have assembled several scenarios for you to use to reach out and contact people that can help you build your business.

Some people you will be able to reach and actually speak with on the first attempt. They may even answer the phone themselves.

Some people you will need to call again.

Some you may never reach, and will just have to leave it at that.

You may choose to leave messages for some of those that you don't reach on the first attempt, but that might be as far as it goes.

In order to talk to some people, you're going to have to talk to a "screener" or their assistant first. Be prepared for this.

In some cases, you won't know the name of the person you need to talk to so you'll have to ask for a position or ask the person who answers your call for the name of the person you should speak with.

You can use the suggested language as I've presented it in this chapter, or you can use it as a guide to develop your own style as you telephone and reach out to people that can help you.

The people you are going to be calling with this strategy will be strangers to you at the moment you contact them — although their name or face might be familiar to you or you might have some common areas of interest.

Therefore, there could be some initial reluctance on their part to take your call, to agree to talk with you, or to want to help you.

Just keep that in mind as you make your calls, but don't let it deter you.

If you don't try these techniques, you're leaving a huge resource of potential leads untapped.

The person you initially contact might have an interest in talking with you about buying or selling, but even more importantly, they can lead you to others.

Again, the telephone call is for the introduction, not a presentation.

Don't Hold Back

Even though you're telephoning strangers, don't use an alias or attempt to disguise who or what you are.

Don't try to block or hide the way your calling information displays on their phone or caller ID.

In fact, make some test calls to another line you have or to a family member to observe the way your information displays. This way you'll know what others are seeing.

Make sure it doesn't say anything like "private number," "blocked," "unknown number," or anything else that hints that you are trying to conceal your identity. Your calls could easily be ignored if that's the case.

Tapping Into A Willingness

People like to help you if they know what you need and feel that it's something they can do.

It's human nature to want to help someone if we feel that we can and that we won't be too inconvenienced by doing so.

You just need to ask the people you're calling for their help and make them aware of what you are looking for

— and be sure to reassure them that they have the ability to help you.

Sometimes you'll wait to address this aspect until a subsequent face-to-face meeting or longer phone call.

Just The Introduction

Remember as you're calling people that you don't know or those who may not recognize your name that you are not selling anything over the phone. You are just establishing an introduction.

Since you're primarily calling other businesses — and occasionally someone after they have given you their number or they have been referred to you — and you are not selling anything, the "no call" regulations should not be a concern. However, check with your particular state just to make sure.

"Do not call" applies to telemarketers, which you are not. You are calling a specific person — though you may not know their name until you connect with them — and you are calling strictly for an introduction. Where it goes from there depends on how the conversation develops.

Call To A Businessperson After An Introductory Letter Has Been Sent

Use this scenario to call any businessperson or

professional after initially sending them a letter of introduction. This is someone you have never met, and they may not have received your letter. If that is the case, go ahead as if this was just a proactive telephone contact. Primarily you want to meet with them to determine what interest they may have in moving and who they know that has an interest in buying a new home. You may have to talk with a receptionist or assistant first.

"Hello. Is <use their first name> in today (available)?"

[If asked the nature of your call, you can mention that you sent them a letter and want to make sure they received it, that you want to introduce yourself, that you'd like to see when they're available to meet with you, or that you would like their help for a minute.]

NOT THERE — [The person you are calling is not present.] *"Do you know when he/she would have a minute for me to call back? This is <your name>. I represent <name of your company or office>."* [Agree on a day and time for the return call.]

"Thanks for your time, and tell <person's name> that I'll call again on <day and time agreed on>. Good-bye."

NOW IS NOT A GOOD TIME — [You actually speak to the person you want to contact and introduce yourself, but they are unable to devote the time to you now.] *"I know that you're busy and that you weren't expecting my call right now. Let me call back when you have a minute."* [Set up a mutually convenient time to talk again.] *"Good-bye."*

HAS JUST A QUICK MINUTE NOW — [You actually get to speak to the person you are calling, but they don't have much time to talk — just set an appointment for the next contact.] *"Great. I'll make this quick. I recently sent you a letter introducing myself and our company. Do you remember receiving it?"* [Wait for response.]

> **Yes, Received It** — *"Great. I wanted to make sure you received it so you'd know who I was when I called to say hello (introduce myself)."*
>
> **No, Did Not Receive** — *"Oh, I'm sorry. I had sent you a letter introducing me and our company so that my name would be familiar to you when I called."*
>
> *"Perhaps it will come in a few days, but I just wanted to take a moment to say hello and introduce myself and <name of your company>."*

"As I mentioned in my letter (had mentioned in the letter that you didn't get), I want to set a time when I could stop by to meet with you and talk for a few minutes."

"I want to learn a little bit more about your business and let you know more about who we are. Plus, I could use your help. Which one is better for you — having me come to your office or letting me buy you a cup of coffee?" [Wait for response.]

[Agree on the place, date, and time.] *"Thanks. I look forward to seeing you on <date of the appointment> at <agreed time> at <agreed location>. Would you like for me to email you a reminder (confirmation)?"* [Wait for response.]

> **Yes** — *"Fine. I'll send you a note on <specific day> to remind you of (confirm) our appointment on <day, time, and location>."*
>
> *"Which email address should I use?"* [Obtain their preferred address and write it down.] *"I look forward to seeing (meeting) you. Good-bye."*
>
> **No** — *"Fine. I'll plan on seeing you then on <mention the day and time> at <place>. Good-bye."*

NOT INTERESTED IN MEETING — [You actually get to speak to the person you are calling, but they do not want to set aside the time to meet with you in-person.] *"That's quite all right. However, I really would like to talk to you some more. I could use your help."*

"May I give you a call in a few days when it's more

convenient?" [Wait for response, and agree on a day and time if possible.]

Agrees To A Call — *"Great. Nice talking with you and I'll call you again <day and time> (in a couple of days). Good-bye."*

Does Not Agree To A Call — [Accomplish what you can on this call.] *"I thought maybe you could help me. That's the primary reason for my call. I'm looking for people who might be looking for a new home now or in the near future — maybe you or someone you know?"*

[If he or she mentions that they have some interest or volunteers a name or two, write it down and ask for a way to contact that person or persons. Be sure to note the correct spelling and pronunciation. Get first names so you don't sound like a telemarketer or solicitor when you call them, and get permission to use the person's name that is giving you the referrals when you contact the other people.]

They have names to give you — *"That's great. I appreciate that and will call them and see how I can help them. Can you think of anyone else?"* [Wait for response.] *"Thanks for your help. Good-bye."*

No names to give you at this time — *"That's quite all right. If you don't mind, I'll check back with you in a few weeks to see if you might be able to help* *me then, and we can take it from there."* [Wait for response.] *"Thanks for your time. Good-bye."*

NOT INTERESTED IN HELPING — [You actually get to speak to the person you are calling, but if there does not seem to be any interest in helping you or in talking with you again, conclude your conversation.] *"Good-bye."*

Call Of Introduction To Area Businesses And Professionals

Use this scenario to call any businessperson or professional without any advance notice of your call or any type of letter introducing yourself. Primarily you want to meet with them to determine any interest level they might have in seeking another home and who they know who might be interested in moving that they can refer to you. You may have to talk with a receptionist or assistant first.

———

"Hello <use their first name or title>? This is <your name> from <name of your company>." [If pressed for the nature of your call, mention that that you want to introduce yourself, that you'd like to see when they're available to meet or talk with you, that you'd like to learn more about their business, or that you would like their help for a minute.]

NOT THERE — [The person you are calling is not present

and you talk to an assistant or someone else.] *"No problem. Do you know when he/she would have a minute for me to call back and introduce myself?"* [Agree on a day and time for the return call.]

"Thanks for your time, and tell <person's name> that I'll call again on <day and time agreed on>. Good-bye."

NOW IS NOT A GOOD TIME — [You actually speak to the person you are calling, but they are unable to devote the time to you now.] *"No problem (That's OK). I know you weren't expecting my call right now. Let me call back when you have a minute to talk with me."* [Set up a convenient time to talk again.] *"Good-bye."*

IS AVAILABLE NOW — [You actually get to speak to the person you want to talk with.] *"Great. I'll make this quick. I just wanted to call to introduce myself and our company and speak to you for a minute. We have never met, but we are your neighbor at <street address, general area, or local landmark>."*

"I'd like to learn a little bit more about your business (clientele) and let you know who we are and what we're doing."

"I'd like to stop by and meet you for a minute, or maybe you'd let me buy you a cup of coffee? Which one works better for you — having me come to your office and meet you there or letting me buy you a cup

of coffee?" [Wait for response.]

[Agree on the place, date, and time.] *"Thanks. I look forward to seeing you on <date of the appointment> at <agreed time> at <location>."*

"Would you like for me to email you a reminder (confirmation)?" [Wait for response.]

Yes — *"Fine. I'll send you a note on <specific day> to remind you of (confirm) our appointment on <day and time>."*

"Which email address should I use?" [Obtain their preferred address and write it down.] *"I look forward to seeing you then. Good-bye."*

No — *"Fine. I'll plan on seeing you then on <day and time> at <place>. Good-bye."*

NOT INTERESTED IN MEETING — [You actually get to speak to the person you are calling, but they do not want to set aside the time to meet with you in-person.] *"That's quite all right. I realize that we've never met and that you are busy. However, I really would like to talk to you some more. I could use your help."*

"When would be a good time for us to spend a couple of minutes on the phone together?" [Wait for response, and agree on a day and time if possible.]

Agrees To A Call — *"Thank you. Nice talking with you and I'll call you again <day and time agreed on> (in a couple of days). Good-bye."*

Does Not Agree To A Call — [Accomplish what you can with them on this call.] *"I thought maybe you could help me. I'm looking to connect with people who might be interested in looking for a new home now or in the near future — maybe you or someone you know?"*

[If he or she mentions that they have some interest or volunteers a name or two, write it down and ask for a way to contact that person or persons. Be sure to note the correct spelling and pronunciation. Get first names so you don't sound like a telemarketer or solicitor when you call them, and get permission to use the person's name that is giving you the referrals when you contact the other people.]

They have names to give you — *"That's great. I will call them and see how I can help. Can you think of anyone else?"* [Wait for response.] *"Thanks for your help. Good-bye."*

No names to give you at this time — *"That's quite all right. If you don't mind, I'll check back with you in a few weeks to see if you might be able to help me then, and we can take it from there."* [Wait for response.]

"Thanks for your time. Good-bye."

NOT INTERESTED IN HELPING — [If there does not seem to be any interest in helping you or in talking with you again, conclude your conversation.] *"Good-bye."*

Call To Social Networking Contact

Use this scenario to call any person that you know of through social networking sites. You are calling without any type of advance notification such as email. You mainly want to talk with them — rather than set a meeting — to determine who they know in your area who has an interest in buying a new home and who they can refer to you — including themself. Call them on their cell phone to avoid office voice mail and "screeners."

———

"Hello <use their first name or title>? This is <your name> from <name of your company>. I saw your profile on <name of networking site where you noticed them and where you are a member also>."

NOW IS NOT A GOOD TIME — [You actually speak to the person you want and introduce yourself, but they are unable to devote the time to you now.] *"No problem. I know you weren't expecting my call right now. Let me call back when you have a minute (when it's more convenient)."* [Set up a convenient time to talk again.] *"Good-bye."*

IS AVAILABLE NOW — [You actually get to speak to the

person you are calling.] *"Great. I'll make this quick. I thought maybe you could help me identify people who might be interested in looking for a new home in my (our) area — now or in the near future."*

[Listen for their general willingness to help you. If he or she mentions that they would like to help, set up another call at a mutually convenient time. If they volunteer a name or two, write it down and ask for a way to contact that person or persons. Be sure to note the correct spelling and pronunciation. Get first names so you don't sound like a telemarketer or solicitor when you call them, and get permission to use the person's name that is giving you the referrals when you contact the other people. If there seems to be no interest in helping you or establishing a professional relationship, conclude the call.] *"Thanks for taking my call. Good-bye."*

Call To Area Business Organizations

Use this scenario to call the executive director, membership director, business development manager, or relocation specialist at a business organization like the Chamber of Commerce, Business Development Board, or Convention and Tourism Bureau to introduce yourself. Some of these groups will already have Realtors® or brokers as members so understand this and be prepared to join the group and become active. You want to meet and identify people who are interested in buying a new home due to transfers, promotions, relocations within the area, expansions, or new businesses coming into your area. Also, you want to become a member, get involved, advertise with them, learn about sponsorships, and display your cards in their office.

––––––

"Hello. Is <use their first name> in today (available)?" [If you don't know the name of the person you should ask for, request the executive director. If pressed for the nature of your call, mention that you would like to join their organization, that you want to introduce yourself, that you might like to advertise on their website, or that you would like his/her help for a minute. If you are connected to someone else, continue your call with that person and learn if they can help you or get referred to the executive director through them.]

[The person you want to talk with is not present.] *"No problem. Do you know when he/she would have a minute (be available) for me to call back?"* [Agree on a day and time for the return call.]

"Thanks for your time, and tell <the person's name> that I'll call again on <day and time agreed on>. Good-bye."

NOW IS NOT A GOOD TIME — [You actually speak to the

person you are calling and are able to introduce yourself to them, but they are unable to devote the time to you now.] *"I know you weren't expecting my call right now, and I apologize for catching you at a busy (inconvenient) time. Let me call back when you have a minute (at a more convenient time)."* [Set up a convenient time to talk again.] *"Good-bye."*

IS AVAILABLE NOW — [The person you are calling can actually talk with you now.] *"Great. I'll make this quick."*

"I just wanted to call to introduce myself and speak to you for a minute. We have never met, but we are your neighbor at <street address, general area, or local landmark>. I'd like to learn a little bit more about your business (clientele, what you're doing) and let you know who we are."

"I'd like to stop by and meet you for a minute, or maybe you'd let me buy you a cup of coffee? Which one is better for you — meeting at your office or letting me buy you a cup of coffee?" [Wait for response.]

[Agree on the place, date, and time.] *"Thanks. I look forward to seeing you on <date of the appointment> at <agreed time> at <location>. Would you like for me to email you a reminder (confirmation)?"* [Wait for response.]

Yes — *"Fine. I'll send you a note on <mention the specific day> to remind you of (confirm) our appointment on <the day and time agreed>."*

"Which email address should I use?" [Obtain their preferred address and write it down.] *"See you then. Good-bye."*

No — *"Fine. I'll plan on seeing you then <day, time, and place agreed upon>. Good-bye."*

NOT INTERESTED IN MEETING — [You actually get to speak to the person you are calling, but they do not want to set aside the time to meet with you in-person — they just want to talk to you now.]

They Will Work With You — *"That's great. Are you aware of anyone right now who is looking for a new home? I love to be able to talk with them."* [Wait for response.]

[If he or she volunteers a name or two, write it down and ask for a way to contact that person or persons. Be sure to note the correct spelling and pronunciation. Get first names so you don't sound like a telemarketer or solicitor, and get permission to use the person's name that is giving you the referrals when you contact the other people.]

"I will call them and see how I can help them.

Thanks for your help. Good-bye."

They Already Have A Relationship — *"I understand. If there's any chance that I could help you or anyone in your organization in the future, I'd like the opportunity."* [Wait for response.] *"Thanks for your help. Good-bye."*

NOT INTERESTED IN HELPING — [If there does not seem to be any interest in helping you or in talking with you again, conclude your conversation.] *"Good-bye."*

Call To Expanding Area Businesses

Use this scenario to call the human resources (HR) director, relocation specialist, or key contact at local businesses that are expanding or hiring — hospital, schools, local government, college or university, manufacturer, research and development, distribution, assembly, transportation, or other business — to meet with them and introduce yourself. Some of them may already have relationships with Realtors® or other brokers. If they do, try to establish yourself as well. You are interested in working with them as their employees are relocating within your area and new ones are coming into the area. Also, you're interested in possibly advertising with them, conducting seminars, or displaying your cards and flyers in their office. You may have to talk to an assistant or a "screener" or make more than one contact before you get the person who you need to talk with.

———

"Hello. Is <use their first name> in today (available)?" [If pressed for the nature of your call, mention that that you want to introduce yourself, that you'd like to offer your congratulations on their success, that you'd like to see when they're available to meet with you, or that you would like their help for a minute. You may only be able to get their assistant.]

Not There — [The person you are calling is not present.] *"Do you know when he/she would have a minute for me to call again?"* [Agree on a day and time for the return call.]

"Thanks for your time, and tell <person's name> that I'll call again on <day and time agreed on>. Good-bye."

Now Is Not A Good Time — [You actually speak to the person you want and introduce yourself, but they are unable to devote the time to you now.] *"I know you're busy and that you weren't expecting my call right now. Let me call back when you have a minute."* [Set up a convenient time to talk again.] *"Goodbye."*

Is Available Now — [The person you are calling can actually talk with you now.] *"Great. I'll make this quick. I just wanted to call to introduce myself and speak to you for a minute. We have never met, but we* are your neighbor at <street address, general area, or local landmark>. I'd like to learn a little bit more about your business (clientele, what you're doing) and let you know who we are."

"I'd like to stop by and meet you for a minute, or maybe you'd let me buy you a cup of coffee? Which one is better for you — meeting at your office or letting me buy you a cup of coffee?" [Wait for response.]

[Agree on the place, date, and time.] "Thanks. I look forward to seeing you on <date> at <agreed time> at <location>. Would you like for me to email you a reminder (confirmation)?" [Wait for response.]

Yes — "Fine. I'll send you a note on <mention the specific day> to remind you of (confirm) our appointment on <day, time, and location>."

"Which email address should I use?" [Obtain their preferred address and write it down.] "I look forward to seeing you then. Good-bye."

No — "Fine. I'll plan on seeing you then on <mention the day and time> at <place>. Good-bye."

NOT INTERESTED IN MEETING — [You actually get to speak to the person you are calling, but they do not want to set aside the time to meet with you in-person.] "I realize that we've never met and that you are busy.

However, I really would like to talk to you some more. I could use your help. When would be a good (convenient) time for us to spend a couple of minutes on the phone together?" [Wait for response, and agree on a day and time if possible.]

Agrees To A Call — *"Thank you. I'll call you again <day and time> (in a couple of days). Good-bye."*

Does Not Agree To A Call — [Accomplish what you can on this call.] *"I thought maybe you could help me. I know that you might already have some relationships with Realtors® or other brokers, but if you're not already working with anyone or there is an opportunity for me to be part of that referral network, I'd like to be able to help you when you are bringing people into our area from out-of-town or you learn of someone here in the company during the normal course of your business who might be looking for a new or different home."* [Wait for response. See if there is an opportunity to work with them and get referrals from them.]

They Will Work With You — *"That's great. Is there anyone right now that you're going to be bringing in or who is relocating to this area that is going to be needing a home — or are you aware of anyone in your organization who might be in the market for a new or different home? Has anyone possibly said anything about wanting to find a new home? I'd love to be able to talk with anyone that comes to mind."*

[Wait for response.]

[If he or she volunteers a name or two, write it down and ask for a way to contact that person or persons. Be sure to note the correct spelling and pronunciation. Get first names so you don't sound like a telemarketer or solicitor, and get permission to use the person's name that is giving you the referrals when you contact the other people.]

"I will call them and see how I can help them and then let you know what I was able to do. Thanks for your help. Good-bye."

They Already Have A Relationship — *"I understand. If there's any chance that I could help you or any of your employees in the future, I'd like the opportunity."* [Wait for response.] *"Thanks for your help. Good-bye."*

NOT INTERESTED IN HELPING — [You actually get to speak to the person you are calling, but they do not seem to be interested in helping you or in talking with you again. Conclude your conversation, and thank them for speaking with you.] *"Good-bye."*

Call To New Or Relocating Businesses

Use this scenario to call the human resources director (HR), relocation specialist, or key contact for a new start-up business or one from outside your market that is relocating or expanding into your area — hospital, college or university, manufacturer, research and development, distribution, assembly, transportation, or other business or employment center — to meet with them and introduce yourself, even if they aren't physically open yet in their new location. Some of them may already have relationships with Realtors® or other brokers. If they do, try to establish yourself as well. You are interested in working with them as their employees are being hired and relocating within your area and as new ones are coming into the area. Also, you're interested in possibly advertising with them, conducting seminars, or displaying your cards and flyers in their office. You may have to talk to an assistant or a "screener" or make more than one contact before you get the person you need to speak to.

———

"Hello. Is <use their first name> in today (available)?" [If pressed for the nature of your call, mention that that you want to introduce yourself, that you'd like to see when they're available to speak or meet with you, that you'd like to welcome them to the area, or that you would like their help for a minute. You may only be able to get their assistant, and you may need to call again.]

NOT THERE — [The person you are calling is not present.] *"Do you know when he/she would have a minute for me to call again and introduce myself?"* [Agree on a day and time for the return call.]

"Thanks for your time, and tell <person's name> that I'll call again on <day and time agreed on>. Good-bye."

NOW IS NOT A GOOD TIME — [You actually speak to the person you are calling and introduce yourself, but they are unable to devote the time to you now.] *"I know you're busy and that you weren't expecting my call right now. Let me call back when you have a minute (when it's more convenient)."* [Set up a convenient time to talk again.] *"Good-bye."*

IS AVAILABLE NOW — [The person you are calling can actually talk with you now.] *"Great. I'll make this quick. We have never met, but we will be your neighbor at <street address, general area, or local landmark>. I'd like to welcome you to our area and learn a little bit more about your business (clientele) — and let you know who we are."*

"I'd like to stop by and meet you for a minute, or maybe you'd let me buy you a cup of coffee?" [You may need to determine when they are going to be in your area if they haven't relocated yet.]

"Which one is better for you — meeting at your office [it may only be a temporary office while their site is being constructed or they still might be selecting their

office location] *or letting me buy you a cup of coffee?"*
[Wait for response.]

[Agree on the place, date, and time]. *"Thanks. I look forward to seeing you on <date of the appointment> at <agreed time> at <location>. Would you like for me to email you a reminder (confirmation)?"* [Wait for response.]

> **Yes** — *"Fine. I'll send you a note on <mention the specific day> to remind you of (confirm) our appointment on <day, time, and location>."*
>
> *"Which email address should I use?"* [Obtain their preferred address and write it down.] *"I look forward to seeing you then. Good-bye."*
>
> **No** — *"Fine. I'll plan on seeing you then on <mention the day and time> at <place>. Good-bye."*

NOT INTERESTED IN MEETING — [You actually get to speak to the person you are calling, but they do not want to set aside the time to meet with you in-person.] *"I realize that we've never met and that you are busy. However, I really would like to talk to you some more. I could use your help. When would be a good time for us to spend a couple of minutes on the phone together?"* [Wait for response, and agree on a day and time if possible.]

Agrees To A Call — *"Thank you. I'll call you again <day*

and time> (in a couple of days). Good-bye."

Does Not Agree To A Call — [Accomplish what you can on this call.] *"I thought maybe you could help me. I know that you might already have some relationships with Realtors® or other brokers, but if you're not already working with anyone or there is an opportunity for me to be part of that referral network, I'd like to be able to help you when you are bringing people into our area from out-of-town or you learn of someone who might be looking for a new or different home in our area."* [Wait for response. See if there is an opportunity to work with them and get referrals from them.]

> **They Will Work With You** — *"That's great. Is there anyone right now who is going to be relocating to this area or moving about within the area that is going to be needing a home — or are you aware of anyone in your company who might be in the market for a different home or possibly is trying to sell their current home? I'd love to be able to talk with them."* [Wait for response.]

[If he or she volunteers a name or two, write it down and ask for a way to contact that person or persons. Be sure to note the correct spelling and pronunciation. Get first names so you don't sound like a telemarketer or solicitor, and get permission to use the person's name that is giving you the

referrals when you contact the other people.]

"I will call them and see how I can help them and let you know how it went. Thanks for your help. Good-bye."

They Already Have A Relationship — *"I understand. If there's any chance that I could help you or any of your employees in the future, I'd like the opportunity."* [Wait for response.] *"Thanks for your help. Good-bye."*

NOT INTERESTED IN HELPING — [You actually get to speak to the person you are calling, but they don't seem to be interested in helping or talking with you again. Conclude your conversation, and thank them for speaking with you.] *"Good-bye."*

Call To Apartment Rental Agents

Use this scenario to call an apartment rental office in your marketplace to introduce yourself, set up a meeting with the manager or leasing agent and discuss how you can help their tenants when they are ready for home ownership — and how they can help you when you need short-term housing for your customers when they must move out of their current home before you are ready to close on their new home that you have sold them. Also, you're interested in possibly advertising with them, conducting seminars, or displaying your cards and flyers in their office.

———

"Hello? Is <use their first name> in today (available)?"
[Ask for the manager, broker, or leasing agent if you
are unsure of a specific name to request. If asked the
nature of your call, you can mention that you'd like to
see about setting an appointment with them.]

NOT THERE — [The person you are calling is not present.]
*"Do you know when he/she would be available for me
to call back?"*

[Agree on a day and time for the return call.] *"Thanks
for your time, and tell <person's name> that I'll call
again on <day and time agreed on>. Good-bye."*

NOW IS NOT A GOOD TIME — [You actually speak to the
person you are calling and introduce yourself, but they
are unable to devote the time to you now.] *"I'm sorry I
caught you at an inconvenient (busy) time, but I want
to discuss a mutually beneficial business relationship
with you. Let me call back when you have a minute
(when it's more convenient)."* [Set up a convenient
time to talk again.] *"Good-bye."*

IS AVAILABLE NOW — [The person you are calling can actually
talk with you now.] *"Great. I'll make this quick. I just
wanted to call to introduce myself and speak to you for a
minute. We have never met, but we are your neighbor at*

<street address, general area, or local landmark>. I'd like to set up a time to meet with you and discuss creating a mutually beneficial business relationship."

"I'd like to stop by and meet you for a minute, or maybe you'd let me buy you a cup of coffee? Which one is better for you — meeting at your office or letting me buy you a cup of coffee?" [Wait for response.]

[Agree on the place, date, and time.] *"Thanks. I look forward to seeing you on <date of the appointment> at <agreed time> at <location>. Would you like for me to email you a reminder (confirmation)?"* [Wait for response.]

> **Yes** — *"Fine. I'll send you a note on <mention the specific day> to remind you of (confirm) our appointment on <day, time, and location>."*
>
> *"Which email address should I use?"* [Obtain their preferred address and write it down.] *"I look forward to seeing you then. Good-bye."*
>
> **No** — *"Fine. I'll plan on seeing you then on <mention the day and time> at <place>. Good-bye."*

NOT INTERESTED IN MEETING — [You actually get to speak to the person you are calling, but they do not want to set aside the time to meet with you in-person.] *"I realize that we've never met and that you are busy.*

However, I really would like to talk to you some more. I could use your help (I think we can help each other, There's an opportunity for us to help each other). When would be a good (convenient) time for us to spend a couple of minutes on the phone together?" [Wait for response, and agree on a day and time if possible.]

Agrees To A Call — *"Thank you. I'll call you again <day and time> (in a couple of days). Good-bye."*

Does Not Agree To A Call — *"I wanted to talk about how we might establish a mutually beneficial business relationship. I think we can help each other."*

[If there seems to be some interest on their part in working with you or hearing what you have to say, pursue setting an appointment to meet or talk more later. If there does not seem to be any interest, conclude your conversation.] *"Good-bye."*

Call To Lenders And Mortgage Brokers

Use this scenario to call a lender, loan officer, or mortgage broker in your marketplace to introduce yourself and discuss opportunities for you to work with people that have come to them to pre-qualify for financing without having a particular new home selected in advance — as well as other people they may know or be aware of who are looking to list their current home or purchase another one. You also want to explore the types of loans they can make to your customers, learn how they are processed, and identify some preferred lenders.

————

"Hello? Is <use their first name> in today (available)?" [If you don't know the name of the person you should ask for, request the manager, broker, or loan officer. If asked the nature of your call, you can mention that you'd like to see when they're available to meet with you (set up an appointment).]

NOT THERE — [The person you are calling is not present.] *"Do you know when he/she would be available for me to call back?"*

[Agree on a day and time for the return call.] *"Thanks for your time, and tell <person's name> that I'll call again on <day and time agreed on>. Good-bye."*

NOW IS NOT A GOOD TIME — [You actually speak to the person you are calling and introduce yourself, but they are unable to devote the time to you now.] *"I'm sorry now is not convenient, but I want to discuss a mutually beneficial business relationship with you. Let me call back when you have a minute."* [Set up a convenient time to talk again.] *"Goodbye."*

IS AVAILABLE NOW — [The person you are calling can

actually talk with you now.] *"Great. I'll make this quick. I'd like to set up a time (convenient time) to meet with you and discuss creating a mutually beneficial business relationship."*

"We can meet at your office, or you could let me buy you a cup of coffee. Which one is better for you?" [Wait for a response.]

[Agree on the place, date, and time.] *"Thanks. I look forward to seeing you on <date of the appointment> at <agreed time> at <location>. Would you like for me to email you a reminder (confirmation)?"* [Wait for response.]

Yes — *"Fine. I'll send you a note on <specific day> to remind you of (confirm) our appointment on <day, time, and location>."*

"Which email address should I use?" [Obtain their preferred address and write it down.] *"I look forward to seeing you then. Goodbye."*

No — *"Fine. Then I'll see you on <day and time agreed> at <place>. Goodbye."*

NOT INTERESTED IN MEETING — [You actually get to speak to the person you are calling, but they do not want to set aside the time to meet with you in-person so go ahead and state your case on this call.] *"I realize that we've never met and that you are busy. However, I'd like to discuss a mutually beneficial business relationship with you. That's why I wanted to meet with you."*

"We can do it by phone if you like. When would be a good time (a convenient time) for us to talk for a few minutes?" [Wait for response, and agree on a day and time if possible.]

Agrees To A Call — *"Thank you. I'll call you again <day and time> (in a couple of days). Good-bye."*

Does Not Agree To A Call — [Accomplish what you can on this call.] *"I wanted to talk about how we might establish a mutually beneficial business relationship."* [If there seems to be some interest, pursue setting an appointment to meet or talk more later. If there does not seem to be any interest, conclude your conversation.] *"Goodbye."*

Call After A Third-Party Visit

Use this scenario to call someone after their proxy (friend, relative, neighbor, trustee, co-worker, or someone else) has visited your office or open house on their behalf to introduce yourself and your company to them and discuss the visit of their proxy. You want to meet with them eventually to help them select their new home. They might be able to lead you to others that have an interest in buying a home in your area also.

———

"Hello <preferably use their first name>? This is <your name> from <name of your company>."

"<Name of their friend, relative, neighbor, co-worker, or representative, and their relationship to the person you are calling — such as 'your Aunt Millie,' or 'your parents,' or 'your friend Sarah from Chicago'> recently stopped by our office (an open house I was hosting) to get some information for you. Have you talked with them since they were here?" [Wait for response.]

No — *"Well, they seemed to like what they saw and thought that it would work well for you (they looked at several ideas for you and seemed to find a couple that they liked that they thought would work for you)."*

"If you like, I can email (mail) you a copy of that floor plan (those homes) for you to review." [Wait for response.]

> **Yes** — *"Fine. Is email OK to use?"* [If not, obtain their mailing address.] *"Which email address should I use?"* [Obtain their preferred address and write it down.]

> *"I'll send it out today and then I'll plan on calling you in a couple of days to go over it with you."* [Arrange a convenient day and time to talk again.] *"I*

look forward to talking to you again you then. Good-bye."

[Wait until the next call to discuss a visit to your office, referrals, or other appropriate action.]

No — *"Fine. I'll plan on talking with you again then on <day, and time>. Good-bye."*

Yes — *"Great. What did they tell you about what they saw?"* [Wait for response.]

POSITIVE OUTLOOK — *"Great, I'm glad to hear that. They seemed to like what they saw and felt that it (one of them) would work well for you."*

"I'd like to set a convenient time to meet with you to let you see for yourself what is available."

[Discuss when they are going to be available or visiting your area and attempt to set up a time to meet. Determine if they need directions.] *"Would you like for me to email you a reminder?"*

> **Yes** — *"Fine. I'll send you a note on <specific day> to remind you of our appointment here on <day and time>."*

> *"Which email address should I use?"* [Obtain their preferred address and write it down.] *"I look*

forward to seeing you then. Good-bye."

No — *"Fine. Then I'll see you here on <day and time>. Goodbye."*

NOT-POSITIVE OUTLOOK — *"Oh, I'm sorry to hear that. What did they tell you about what they saw?"*

[Listen without interrupting and address their concerns as simply as you can without going into unnecessary detail or trying to conduct a mini-presentation. Remember you just want to set an appointment. You are not trying to make the sale over the phone.]

[Conduct a limited amount of discovery to learn what they desire and approximately when they would like to occupy it. Then go for setting the appointment.]

"You really need to see for yourself what opportunities are available. After all, you're the ultimate judge of what you're looking for and what's going to work for you. Maybe you'll find something that you really like. You won't know until you see for yourself."

[If they agree with you, set a convenient time to meet on-site or at least talk again.] *"Would you like for me to email you a reminder?"* [Wait for response.]

Yes — *"Fine. I'll send you a note on <specific day>*

to remind you of our appointment here on <day and time>."

"Which email address should I use?" [Obtain their preferred address and write it down.] *"I look forward to seeing you then. Good-bye."*

No — *"Fine. Then I'll see you here on <day and time>. Good-bye."*

NOT INTERESTED IN VISITING — [When you actually get to speak to the person you are calling, but their interest is weak or they do not want you to contact them again, go for a referral.]

"I appreciate your interest in looking at homes in our area and for having your <relationship of people who contacted you, such as parents or friend> take a look at something for you, and I'm sorry that you don't think we can help you, but I'm just curious. You must have thought our home (properties) was/were worth checking out or you wouldn't have had your friend (parents, cousins, co-worker) visit us for you, so let me ask you a question."

"Who can you think of who might be looking for a new home or might like to look at what we can show them?" [Wait for response.]

They Have Names To Give You — *"Great. I'll be glad*

to contact them and invite them to take a look at what we have to offer (see how I can help them)."

[If he or she volunteers a name or two, write it down and ask for a way to contact them. Be sure to note the correct spelling and pronunciation. Get first names so you don't sound like a telemarketer or solicitor when you call, and get permission to use the person's name that is giving you the referrals when you contact the other people. You may have to request this information in writing by mail or email to establish credibility.] *"Thanks for your help, and good luck in your search for a new home. If I can be of any assistance, please call me. Good-bye."*

No Names To Give You At This Time — *"That's quite all right. I appreciate your help and the interest you've shown in the homes (properties) I represent. Good luck in your search for a new home. If I can be of any assistance, please call me. Good-bye."*

Call To Remodelers And Contractors

Use this scenario to call a remodeler, handyman, or contractor (roofing, siding, pool, landscaping, electrical, painting, plumbing, HVAC, carpentry, flatwork) who has done work or who is doing work in your immediate market that you have identified from their yard signs or vehicles — to introduce yourself and discuss homes that they're working on that might be getting ready to be listed (either with an agent on by the owner) and to create a professional relationship for referrals back and forth because you may need to recommend a remodeler or handyman to your clients.

"Hello <use their first name>?" [The person you're calling may answer or there might be a receptionist or someone else that will answer.]

NOT THERE — [The person you are calling is not present.] *"Do you know when he/she would be available for me to call back and speak with him/her?"* [If pressed for the nature of your call, mention that that you want to introduce yourself, that you'd like to see when they're available to meet or talk with you, or that you would like their help for a minute.]

[Agree on a day and time for the return call.] *"Thanks for your time. Tell <person's name> that I'll call again on <day and time agreed on>. Good-bye."*

NOW IS NOT A GOOD TIME — [You actually speak to the person you are calling and introduce yourself, but they are unable to devote the time to you now.] *"I'm sorry now is not a convenient (good) time for you to talk, but I want to discuss a mutually beneficial business relationship with you. Let me call back when you have a minute (when it's more convenient)."* [Set up a convenient time to talk again.] *"Good-bye."*

IS AVAILABLE NOW — [The person you are calling can actually talk with you now.] *"Great. I'll make this quick. I've noticed that you've been doing some work in the <name of the neighborhood> area/on <name of street>, and I'd like to meet or talk with you about creating a strategic alliance between us (and I think we can help each other)."*

"Which one is better for you — to meet at your office or let me buy you a cup of coffee?" [Wait for a response.] [Agree on the place, date, and time.] *"Thanks."*

"I look forward to seeing you on <date of the appointment> at <agreed time> at <location>. Would you like for me to email you a reminder (confirmation)?" [Wait for response.]

   Yes — *"Fine. I'll send you a note on <specific day> to remind you of (confirm) our appointment on <day, time, and location>."*

   "Which email address should I use?" [Obtain their preferred address and write it down.] *"I look forward to seeing you then. Good-bye."*

   No — *"Fine. Then I'll see you on <day and time> at <place>. Good-bye."*

NOT INTERESTED IN MEETING — [You actually get to speak to the person you are calling, but they do not want to set aside the time to meet with you in-person.] *"I realize that we've never met and that you are busy. However, I'd like to discuss a mutually beneficial business relationship with you. That's why I wanted to meet with you."*

"We can do it by phone if you like. When would be a good (convenient) time for us to talk for a few minutes?" [Wait for response, and agree on a day and time if possible.]

Agrees To A Call — *"Thank you. I'll call you again <day and time> (in a couple of days). Good-bye."*

Does Not Agree To A Call — [Accomplish what you can on this call.] *"I wanted to talk about how we might establish a mutually beneficial business relationship."*

[If there seems to be some interest, pursue setting an appointment to meet or talk more later. If there does not seem to be any interest, conclude your conversation.] *"Good-bye."*

Call To Brokers You've Never Met

Use this scenario to call the broker in neighboring realty offices in your market area to introduce yourself and discuss creating a strategic alliance with them to help sell your homes, for referrals, and for exchanging information.

———

"Hello <use the first name of the broker>?" [The person you're calling may answer, or there might be a receptionist or someone else in the office that will answer. If you don't know the specific name of the person you are calling, request the broker or office manager.]

NOT THERE — [The person you want is not present.] *"Do you know when he/she would be available for me to call back?* [If pressed for the nature of your call, mention that that you want to introduce yourself, that you'd like to see when they're available to meet or talk with you, or that you would like their help for a minute.]

[Agree on a day and time for the return call.] *"Thanks for your time, and tell <person's name> that I'll call again on <day and time agreed on>. Good-bye."*

NOW IS NOT A GOOD TIME — [You actually speak to the person you are calling and introduce yourself, but they are unable to devote the time to you now.] *"I'm sorry now is not convenient, but I want to discuss a mutually beneficial business relationship with you. Let me call back when you have a minute."* [Set up a convenient time to talk again.] *"Goodbye."*

IS AVAILABLE NOW — [The person you are calling can actually talk with you now.] *"Great. I'll make this quick. I don't think we've ever met before, but I wanted to call and introduce myself."*

"I'd like to set up a time to meet with you and discuss creating a mutually beneficial business relationship."

"We can meet at your office, or maybe you'd let me buy you a cup of coffee. Which is better for you?" [Wait for a response.]

[Agree on the place, date, and time.] *"Thanks. I look forward to seeing you on <date of the appointment> at <agreed time> at <location>. Would you like for me to email you a reminder (confirmation)?"* [Wait for response.]

> **Yes** — *"Fine. I'll send you a note on <the specific day> to remind you of (confirm) our appointment on <agreed day, time, and location>."*
>
> *"Which email address should I use?"* [Obtain their preferred address and write it down.] *"I look forward to seeing you then. Goodbye."*
>
> **No** — *"Fine. Then I'll see you on <mention the day and time> at <place>. Goodbye."*

NOT INTERESTED IN MEETING — [You actually get to speak to the person you are calling, but they do not want to set aside the time to meet with you.] *"I realize that we've never met and that you are busy. However, I'd like to discuss a mutually beneficial business relationship with you. That's why I wanted to meet with you."*

"We can do it by phone if you like. When would be a good time for us to talk for a few minutes?"

[Wait for response, and agree on a day and time if possible.]

Agrees To A Call — *"Thank you. I'll call you again <day and time> (in a couple of days). Good-bye."*

Does Not Agree To A Call — [Accomplish what you can on this call.] *"I wanted to talk about how we might establish a mutually beneficial business relationship."*

[If there seems to be some interest, pursue setting an appointment to meet or talk more later. If there does not seem to be any interest, conclude your conversation.] *"Goodbye."*

Call To Realtors® With A Listing In Your Area

Use this scenario to call any Realtor® who has an active listing in your marketplace to introduce yourself and your company and create a professional relationship for co-broking and the exchange of information.

———

"Hello <use the first name of the Realtor® with the listing>?" [Use their cell phone number that you get from the yard sign.] *"This is <your name> of <name of*

company or office>."

NOW IS NOT A GOOD TIME — [You actually speak to the person you are calling and get to introduce yourself, but they are unable to devote the time to you now.] *"I'm sorry now is not convenient (a good time), but I wanted to introduce myself to you and learn about the property you have listed in case I can help you find a buyer. Let me call back when you have a minute (when it's more convenient)."* [Set up a convenient time to talk again.] *"Goodbye."*

IS AVAILABLE NOW — [The person you are calling can actually talk with you now.] *"Great. I'll make this quick. I don't believe we have ever met so I wanted to call to introduce myself and learn a little bit more about the home you have listed at <actual street address> in <neighborhood, subdivision, or area>. This is my market area (my market area, too) and perhaps I can find a buyer for you."*

"I'd like to stop by your office and meet you for a minute, or maybe you'd let me buy you a cup of coffee? Which one is better for you — meeting at your office or letting me buy you a cup of coffee?" [Wait for response.]

[Agree on the place, date, and time.] *"Thanks. I look forward to seeing you on <date> at <agreed time> at <location>. Would you like for me to email you a* *reminder (confirmation)?"* [Wait for response.]

Yes — *"Fine. I'll send you a note on <specific day> to remind you of (confirm) our appointment on <day, time, and location>."*

"Which email address should I use?" [Obtain their preferred address and write it down.] *"I look forward to seeing you then. Good-bye."*

No — *"Fine. Then I'll see you on <day and time> at <place>. Good-bye."*

NOT INTERESTED IN MEETING — [You actually get to speak to the person you are calling, but they do not want to set aside the time to meet with you in-person.] *"I realize that we've never met and that you are busy. However, I just wanted to say hello and let you know that I will try to find a buyer for your listing."*

[If there does not seem to be any interest in working with you or pursuing a professional relationship, conclude your conversation.] *"Good-bye."*

Call To "FSBO"

Use this scenario to call a homeowner that has a "For Sale By Owner" sign in their yard. **Assure them that you are not trying to list their home or talk them out of selling it themselves** — because they likely have had several Realtors® already approach them. You want to talk with or meet them because this is your market area, you are curious about the interest they've had in their home, you want to sell them their next home if they haven't selected it yet, and you want to know who else they know who might be interested in moving. You will be using the telephone number that is listed on the sign.

———

"Hello? I saw your 'For Sale' sign. Are you the homeowner?" [If not, ask for the homeowner or determine when you can call back and speak to them — but be prepared for resistance or reluctance when you begin your call. You might be treated like a telemarketer. If asked if you are a Realtor®, answer the question, but reiterate that you are calling about their sign.] *"I'm <your name> of <name of your company or office>."*

NOW IS NOT A GOOD TIME — [You speak to the person you want, but they really can't talk with you now.] *"I'm sorry that now is not convenient, but I just had a couple of questions for you. Let me call back when you have a minute (at a more convenient time)."* [Set up a convenient time to talk again.] *"Goodbye."*

IS AVAILABLE NOW — [The person you are calling can actually talk with you now.] *"Great. We've never met, but I wanted to ask you a quick question since I noticed that your home is on the market and that you are selling it yourself."*

"By the way, who am I speaking with, please?" [If they offer their name, great, if not, continue with the conversation anyway. You don't need their name except to personalize the conversation.]

"I'm not calling about listing your present home, but I was wondering if you already have made a decision on your next home?" [Wait for response.]

Yes, Purchased — *"That's great. Can you tell me what you have selected?"* [Listen for their response and congratulate them on their decision.] *"That sounds like a lovely home."*

"I'm just curious. Do you know anyone else — maybe a neighbor, relative, co-worker, or friend — who has mentioned that they are thinking of (planning on) selling their home or finding another one that I might be able to talk with?" [Wait for response.]

They Have Names To Give You — *"Great. I'll be glad to contact them."* [Write down the names with the correct spelling and pronunciation. Be sure to obtain first names. Find out how to contact them, the preferred method of contact, and the exact contact information. Get permission to use their name. You may have to request this information in writing by mail or email to establish credibility. Be sensitive to their privacy and accommodate their wishes if this is the case.] *"Thanks for your help,* *and good luck in your new home."*

No Names To Give You At This Time — *"That's quite all right. Thanks for taking my call. If you think of anyone later and want to call me, that'll be fine. May I email you my contact information?"* [Wait for their response and accept the answer, either way.]

"Good luck in your new home."

"Oh, one more thing. If I find someone interested in possibly purchasing your home, would you be willing to pay me a professional services fee (commission) if they decide to buy your home?" [Wait for response. Thank them either way and conclude your conversation.] *"Good-bye."*

No Decision Yet — *"I'd love to meet with you to find out what you have in mind for your next home"* [provided you have determined that they are staying in the area and purchasing again rather than renting or making other arrangements]. *"Then I can determine some homes for you to consider that meet your criteria."* [Wait for response. Set up a convenient day and time to meet if they are agreeable. Determine the location — their home, your office, or a coffee shop.]

"Fine. Then I will plan on seeing you here (there, at <name of location>) on <day and date> at <time>. I'm putting it on my calendar right now."

"By the way, my telephone number is <office number> (<cell number>,<both numbers>). Our website is <web address> if you'd like a little more information about us before we meet. Would you like for me to email you my contact information or a reminder (confirmation) of the visit?" [Wait for response.]

> **Yes** — *"Fine. I'll send you a note (my contact information, my contact information and a note) on <the specific day> to remind you of (confirm) our appointment here (there, <name of location>) on <day and time>."* [Determine if they need directions.]
>
> *"Which email address should I use?"* [Obtain it and write it down.] *"I look forward to seeing you then. Good-bye."*
>
> **No** — *"Fine. Then I'll see you here on <day and time>. Good-bye."*

NO INTEREST IN MEETING — *"That's all right. I appreciate you taking a couple of minutes to talk with me. Good luck on the sale of your home and in finding a new one. If I can help you in any way, please call me."*

"Oh, one more thing. If I find someone interested in possibly purchasing your home, would you be willing to pay me a professional services fee (commission) if they decide to buy your home?" [Wait for response. Thank them either way and conclude your conversation.] *"Good-bye."*

Call To Existing Owners

Use this scenario to call a homeowner in your market area to introduce yourself and learn if they might be thinking of listing their present home or getting another one — as well as who they know that you could talk with about buying or selling. Make sure that you know their name and check the "no call list" first as a precaution.

———

"Hello <preferably use their first name>? This is <your name> from <name of your company or office>. We have never met, but I sell real estate in <name of that community, neighborhood, or area>. Do you have a moment to talk?" [Wait for response.]

NOW IS NOT A GOOD TIME — [They are busy now.] *"I'm sorry now is not convenient for you. I wanted to say hello and introduce myself. Let me call back at a better (more convenient) time."* [Set up a more convenient time to talk.] *"Good-bye."*

IS AVAILABLE NOW — [They can actually talk with you now.] *"Great. I'll make this quick. I wanted to introduce myself and make you aware that I am here to help you if you ever decide to sell your present home or look for another one."* [Wait for response.]

Definite Or Some Interest — *"Great. I'd love to talk with you about your plans and see how I can help you.*

When is a convenient time for us to talk again or meet for a cup of coffee?" [Set up a convenient day and time for the next phone call or meeting.]

"Which one is best for you — to talk by phone, to meet at my office, or to let me buy you a cup of coffee?" [Wait for a response.]

[Agree on the place, date, and time.] *"Thanks. I look forward to seeing you on <date of the appointment> at <agreed time> at <location> (I look forward to speaking with you on <date of the appointment> at <agreed time> and I will call you then). Would you like for me to email you a reminder (confirmation)?"* [Wait for response.]

> **Yes** — *"Fine. I'll send you a note on <specific day> to remind you of (confirm) our appointment on <day, time, and location> (our telephone call on <day and time >)."*

> *"Which email address should I use?"* [Obtain it and write it down.] *"I look forward to seeing (talking with) you then. Good-bye."*

> **No** — *"Fine. Then I'll see you on <day and time> at <place> (Then I'll call you on <day and time>). Good-bye."*

No Interest — *"I understand, but I'd like to ask you for* *a small favor. I know you might be aware of people who have mentioned that they are thinking of selling their present home or buying another one."*

"Who can you think of that might apply to that I should talk with about how I might be able to help them?"

They Have Names To Give You — *"Great. I'll be glad to contact them."* [Write down the names with the correct spelling and pronunciation. Be sure to obtain first names. Find out how to contact them, the preferred method of contact, and the exact contact information. Get permission to use their name. You may have to request this information in writing by mail or email to establish credibility. Be sensitive to their privacy and accommodate their wishes if this is the case.] *"Thanks for your help. Good-bye."*

No Names To Give You At This Time — *"That's quite all right. Thanks for taking my call. If you think of anyone later and want to call me, that'll be fine. May I email you my contact information?"* [Wait for their response and accept the answer, either way.] *"Good-bye."*

Call To A Solicitation

Use this scenario to call someone (not a company but a specific person for whom you have a name and phone number or to call back an unknown number from a missed call) who has solicited you for their business — a flyer left on your windshield, a magnet stuck to your car door, an unsolicited email, a direct mail flyer or postcard, a coupon or other mailing you received, or a missed call or voice mail message from a number unfamiliar to you — to turn the tables on them and reach out to them to introduce yourself and find out if they might be interested in selling their present home or getting another one or who they might know that you could talk with that might be so inclined.

———

"Hello <use their first name>? This is <your name> from <name of your company>. We have never met, but I received a flyer (email, calendar magnet, coupon, postcard, mailing, call) from you (from someone at this number) about your business (opportunity, special offer, discount)." [Assume that this is a good time for them to talk with you since they are soliciting your business. Proceed as if they are agreeing to talk with you now unless they interrupt you and mention that now is not a good time for them to talk for even a couple of minutes.]

"While I am intrigued by your offer [if you are] *and I thank you for reaching out to me, I really wanted to call to introduce myself and tell you that I have an opportunity also that perhaps you could take advantage of."* or *"While I am not currently in the market for <name*

or general description of the product or service that they
are offering> I wanted to thank you for reaching out to
me. I also want to introduce myself to you and tell you
that I have an opportunity as well that perhaps you could
take advantage of." [Wait for response.]

"I'd love to talk with you some more on the phone or
over coffee. Maybe I can help you with your business,
and there's a possibility you can help me with mine."

"Which one is better for you — to talk again or to let
me buy you a cup of coffee?" [Wait for a response.]

[Agree on the place, date, and time.] "Thanks. I look
forward to seeing you on <date of the appointment> at
<agreed time> at <location>." **or** "I look forward to
talking with you again on <date of the appointment>
at <agreed time>. I will call you then."

"Would you like for me to email you a reminder
(confirmation)?" [Wait for response.]

   Yes — "Fine. I'll send you a note on <specific day>
   to remind you of (confirm) our appointment on
   <day, time, and location>."

   "Which email address should I use?" [Obtain their
   preferred address and write it down.] "I look
   forward to seeing (talking with) you then. Good-
   bye."

No — *"Fine. Then I'll see (talk with) you on <day and time> at <place>. Good-bye."*

No Interest In Helping — *"That's all right. I appreciate you taking a couple of minutes to talk with me. Good luck on your business. If I can help you in any way, please call me."*

Call With A Solicitation

Use this scenario when someone calls you to discuss an opportunity with you that you did not request or expect — to turn the tables on them and reach out to them to introduce yourself and find out if they might be interested in buying or selling a home or who they might know that you could talk with about finding a home.

[After they introduce themselves and mention why they are calling, ask for their name and write it down. Note the correct spelling. They won't be expecting this and it will throw them off their script or pitch. Then you can take control of the conversation.]

"I am so glad you called although I really wasn't expecting to hear from you. While I am intrigued by your offer [if you are], you should know that I have an opportunity, too, that perhaps you could take advantage of (might be interested in)." **or** *"I am so glad you called, and while I am not currently in the market*

for <name or general description of the product or service that they are offering> thanks for reaching out to me. I also want tell you that I have an opportunity as well that perhaps you could take advantage of (might be interested in)." [Wait for response. They may hang up at this point because you will have gained the upper hand in the conversation. They might pursue it with you though.]

"I'd love to talk with you some more on the phone when I'm not so busy. Maybe I can help you with your business, and there's a possibility you can help me with mine."

"What is a good time and day for us to talk again?" [Wait for a response and agree on the date and time — if the caller hasn't decided to end the call.] *"Thanks."*

"I look forward to talking with you again on <date of the appointment> at <agreed time>. I will call you then."

"Would you like for me to email you a reminder (confirmation)?" [Wait for response.]

    Yes — *"Fine. I'll send you a note on <specific day> to remind you of (confirm) our appointment on <day and time>."*

    "Which email address should I use?" [Obtain it and write it down.] *"I look forward to talking with you then. Good-bye."*

No — *"Fine. Then I'll talk with you again on <day and time>. Good-bye."*

No Interest In Helping — *"That's all right. I appreciate you taking a couple of minutes to talk with me. Good luck on your business. If I can help you in any way, please call me."*

Leaving A Voice Mail Message

Use this scenario whenever you attempt to contact someone by phone to introduce yourself or your company and you get their voice mail or an answering machine (whether it's their landline or cell phone doesn't matter). Just leave the following message — and only on the initial call. Remember that the reason for the call is the introduction, but it is polite to leave the message. Don't expect a return call.

———

"Hi <use their first name>, this is <your name>. I don't think we've ever met, but I'm with <name of your company and/or office>."

"I was calling to introduce myself to you. I know of you through <mention the specific club or organization that you have in common, such as chamber of commerce, church, Little League, Rotary Club, PTA, civic group, association, social media site, etc.>." *("We are your neighbor at <street address, general*

area, or local landmark>)." [You can also mention a mutual friend or associate who recommended that you contact this person.]

[If you don't know of them other than seeing their name on a sign, billboard, ad, flyer, or vehicle, just mention that you saw their name and where you saw it.]

"I'm sorry to have called when you weren't available. I'll try again another time, but my number here is <telephone number>. I'd like to set up a convenient time when you have a couple of minutes when I could stop by and meet you, or perhaps you'd let me buy you a cup of coffee. Thank you. Goodbye."

[This should not appear to be totally unsolicited or a sales call. It should sound like the outreach call that it is. You may try calling again, but do not leave any more messages if you do not reach the person you're calling.]

[If you get a voice mail prompt on subsequent calls, hang up before the "beep" on their voice messaging system starts the recording. Don't worry about your number showing up on their "caller ID."

[If they call back because they see that they have missed a call and don't recognize the number, you'll get to speak with them and introduce yourself at that time — the objective for calling them in the first place.]

Leaving A Message With An Assistant

Use this scenario whenever you attempt to contact a businessperson or professional by phone to introduce yourself and your company and you get their assistant (not a "screener" or receptionist unless they happen to be their personal assistant) rather than a voice mail or an answering machine. Just leave the following message — and only on the initial call. Remember that the reason for the call is the introduction. Don't provide a lot of details and don't expect a return call.

———

"This is <your name>. I'm calling for <name of person you're calling>. He/she may not know me (recognize my name); I don't think we've ever met."

"I'm with <name of your company> and the reason for my call is to introduce myself and our company and to discuss a way I think we could help each other. I know of him/her through <mention the specific club or organization that you have in common, such as an association, chamber of commerce, church, Little League, Rotary Club, PTA, etc.>." ("A mutual friend recommended that I contact him/her.") ("We are your neighbor at <street address, general area, or local landmark>.")

[It should sound like there is a real purpose to your call and not just a random unsolicited call without any foundation.] *"I'll try again another time to reach him/her. Do you know when he/she might be available?"*

[Wait for response and agree on a day and time to call again.] *"Thank you. Good-bye."*

[If the receptionist or assistant wants you to leave your phone number or a more detailed message, politely decline because it is unlikely you will ever get a return call. Insist that you'll try again later. If you get the same results on subsequent calls, scratch this person from your list, or drop into their office to try to see them in-person and start a conversation.]

[You may try calling again, but do not leave a second message — just your name. If the receptionist or assistant begins to recognize your voice, it's time to stop because you are not going to make the connection.]

Call Back From A Message

While it is highly unlikely that you will ever get a call back from a voice mail message you leave for someone you are attempting to make an introduction and potential relationship with, it's possible that their assistant will call you for more information — whether or not you originally spoke to the assistant. Treat this opportunity the same as your original call and make the most of securing the introduction and opening the door for future discussions.

[After the person calling you identifies themself as the person you were calling or the assistant to that person and they ask for more information about the nature of your call and your business, you can begin your explanation.] *"As I mentioned in my voice message, I'm with <name of your company> and I was calling to introduce myself and our company and to discuss a way I think we could help each other. I know of him/her/you through <mention the specific club or organization that you have in common, such as the chamber of commerce, church, Rotary Club, PTA, Little League, Scouts, other youth activities, an association, etc.>."* *("A mutual friend recommended that I contact him/her/you.")* *("We are your neighbor at <street address, general area, or local landmark>.")*

"When would be a good (convenient) time for us (he/she and I) to talk for a few minutes?" [Wait for response, and agree on a day and time if possible.]

Agrees To A Call — *"Thank you. I'll call you again <day and time> (in a couple of days). Good-bye."*

Does Not Agree To A Call — [Accomplish what you can on this call.] *"I wanted to talk with you (him/her) about how we might establish a mutually beneficial business relationship to refer business to each other. I think that I can help you (your company), and you can possibly help me."* [If there seems to be some interest, pursue setting an appointment to meet or talk more later. If there does not seem to be any interest, conclude your conversation.] *"Goodbye."*

Call From A Flyer, Ad, Or Website

When you get a call back from a flyer, direct mail piece, ad, your website, or listing on an online social site, make the most of introducing yourself, selling your company and capabilities, determining their needs, setting an appointment, and getting referrals.

———

[After the person calling you identifies themself and the reason for their call, begin to obtain information on what they are looking for and how you can help them. They may be calling about a specific listing for pricing or feature information. They might be calling to get ideas about selling their home or general information on real estate activity in your area. They may be trying to determine an agent to work with or deciding if now is a good time to buy or sell. They may be inquiring about short sales or a pre-foreclosure. Discuss what you can and try to set an appointment to meet if they seem serious about going ahead with listing or buying.]

"I'd love to meet with you to learn more about what you have in mind, and go over some ideas (homes) that meet your criteria that we can then go look at together." [Wait for response. Set up a convenient day and time to meet if they are agreeable. Determine the

location — their home, your office, or a coffee shop — and who will be present at the meeting.]

NO INTEREST IN MEETING — *"Fine. Then I will plan on seeing you (you and your husband, wife, friend, mother) here (there, at <name of location>) on <day and date> at <time>. I'm putting it on my calendar right now."*

"Would you like for me to email you my contact information or a reminder (confirmation) of the visit?" [Wait for response.]

Yes — *"Fine. I'll send you a note (my contact information, my contact information and a note) on <the specific day> to remind you of (confirm) our appointment here (there, <name of location>) on <day and time>."* [Determine if they need directions.]

"Which email address should I use?" [Obtain it and write it down.] *"I look forward to seeing you then. Good-bye."*

No — *"Fine. Then I'll see you here on <day and time>. Good-bye."*

NO INTEREST IN MEETING — *"That's all right. I appreciate you calling and talking with me. Good luck on the sale of your home* [if they have said that they will be selling their current home or if it's already on the market] *and in finding a new one. If I can help you in any way, please call me."*

[If they indicate that they are selling their home without a Realtor®]*"By the way, if I find someone interested in possibly purchasing your home, would you be willing to pay me a professional services fee (commission) if they decide to buy your home?"* [Wait for response. Thank them either way and conclude your conversation.]

"Oh, one more thing. I know you might be aware of people who have mentioned that they are thinking of selling their present home or buying another one. Who can you think of that might apply to that I should talk with about how I might be able to help them?"

They Have Names To Give You — *"Great. I'll be glad to contact them."* [Write down the names with the correct spelling and pronunciation. Be sure to obtain first names. Find out how to contact them, the preferred method of contact, and the exact contact information. Get permission to use their name. You may have to request this information in writing by mail or email to establish credibility. Be sensitive to their privacy and accommodate their wishes if this is the case.] *"Thanks for your help. Good-bye."*

No Names To Give You At This Time — *"That's quite all right. Thanks for calling me. If you think of anyone later and want to call me back, that'll be fine. May I email you my contact information?"* [Wait for their response and accept the answer, either way.] *"Good-bye."*

6

Approaching
People In Writing

The Power Of Letters

To reach out to strangers, face-to-face and telephone introductions are very useful — and they are effective in many situations.

However, sometimes it's going to take a written message to make a connection or at least attempt to connect with someone — especially someone who does not know you, possibly has never heard of you or your company, probably has not planned on hearing from you, and likely didn't know that you want them to do business with you.

Sometimes, writing is the method of choice.

Written communication isn't always quicker or as

efficient as talking to someone in-person or by telephone, but in working with people you have never met, the written word can establish credibility and a sense of formality more effectively than the other methods.

It's important to have a strategy that enables you to use all three means of contact — in-person, written, and telephone.

A More Formal Approach

When working with people who are strangers to you at the time of writing — even though you might know them by sight or their name is familiar to you — stay away from the email approach.

While that can work for people you know, when you are introducing yourself to strangers or business people you have not met, an informal approach is not acceptable.

Your written introduction needs to set a business tone, and it needs to be a typed (computer generated letter) letter unless it is a high-quality commercially purchased congratulations card or notecard.

Emails just are not appropriate for an initial contact with someone you do not know, and they should be avoided for this reason.

It's unlikely an unsolicited email would even be seen.

When you are sending a letter of introduction, you can also include your business card, tri-folds, reprints, financing rate cards, or other information if you feel they enhance your message for the person you are contacting.

However, try to keep the initial contact brief and on-point. Save most of the collaterals until subsequent contacts.

A Reasonable First Step

In many cases, written contact is the easiest proactive or intentional contact because it doesn't require you to go anywhere or speak to anyone.

There is nothing to prepare except the name and address of the person you are contacting.

It doesn't depend on someone being available at the exact same time that you are. No appointments are necessary, and there are no receptionists or "screeners" to go through.

Reaching outside your comfort zone shouldn't be an issue either. You have plenty of time to think of what to say before sending your letter.

After your initial written contact, then you can follow

with a phone call or email.

Letters Require Less Effort

Another nice aspect of written contact is that is can be essentially the same message for everyone that you want to contact in a specific group of occupations or settings.

In addition, no one will be answering back so there are no planned answers or responses to prepare or rehearse in advance — either in writing or verbally.

Without the physical trip to their location or calling and attempting to reach them on the phone, written contact requires less effort on your part to be intentional.

The drawback is that you won't know if your letter or card that you sent has been received and read — and what the person receiving the letter or card might think about you contacting them — without an additional step by you.

In this chapter, I've assembled some examples of letters and a few cards — but no emails — that you can use as you contact people that you want to reach out to proactively and intentionally.

Some of the people that you are going to want to reach out to, you will know by name or appearance from having seen them in your market area or at public events you've attended. However, others will not be familiar to you at all.

Letters Are Only One Approach

Remember that the reason you are using the letter, or in a few cases a card, is to communicate when a personal approach is not practical or necessary.

This does not take the place of actually speaking to someone. It is just an alternate first step in contacting someone that you don't know.

Use these suggested letters and cards exactly as they are or modify them for your personal writing style. Do not attempt to have the letters do more than they are designed to do.

They are for introductions only, and you can enclose some information about your properties or company. However, they should not have a strong sales message.

You will still have to speak to people on the phone or in-person to discuss their listing, show homes to them, and get the referrals from them that you are seeking.

Your Signature Block

In the interest of keeping the following examples of

letters as short as possible — showing just the salutation and main body of the letter — the following information (even if you already have mentioned it elsewhere in the body of the letter, such as your phone number, email address, or website) should be added after the text of each message as a way of closing the letter:

> *Sincerely,*
> <space>
> *<Company name>*
> <space>
> *<Your signature>*
> <space>
> *<Your name — as you want your customers to call you — plus any professional designations you use>*
> *<Your position or title>*
> *<Your direct office phone line or extension>*
> *<Your fax number>*
> *<Your cell phone number>*
> *<Your email address>*
> *<Your company website address>*
> *<Your company blog address>*
> <space>
> *<Your company "tagline">*
> <space>
> *<Any attachments or enclosures>*

For handwritten notes only, just sign them legibly in

your own hand — use your first and last name — and omit listing all the other contact information. Enclose a business card to supply the other contact information — even if some of it is printed elsewhere on the card.

The Inside Address

Depending on who is the subject of your letter and whether you are sending it to them at their office or residence, you would use some or all of the following for each letter (except for notes), plus the *<Date>* which would appear at the top before the inside address:

> *<Name, including any professional designations>*
> *or <Names, if a couple>*
> *<Title or Position, if applicable>*
> *<Name of Business, if sent to the business>*
> *<Business Address, including department, suite number, floor, or building, if sent to the business>*
> *<Home Address, including apartment number, if sent to the residence>*
> *<City, State, Zip>*

Letter To People In The News

Use this letter to contact someone because of an article about them you saw online or in your local newspaper — or even news that you heard on TV. Only do this if you know their first and last name and can get a mailing address for them. A "Dear Mr. Johnson" or "Dear Award

Winner" just isn't going to work. In addition to introducing you and your company, your letter acknowledges and congratulates their achievement, and it opens the door for a potential discussion with them about finding a new home and for referrals.

———

Dear <name of person in the news>,

Congratulations on being named (honored, recognized) as <position, accomplishment, achievement, promotion, award, honor, designation, or office>.

Although we have never met, I hope you will accept my sincere best wishes on this honor (achievement).

If you think that you will be looking for a new home in the near future, I would enjoy speaking to you about helping you find that ideal home.

I can be reached at <phone number> or <email>, and you can learn more us at <website address>.

All of us here at <name of your company> join in applauding (celebrating) your accomplishment (award, achievement, honor).

Handwritten Note To People In The News

Use this handwritten note to contact someone because

of an article about them you saw online or in your local newspaper — or even news that you heard on TV. Only do this if you know their complete first (not just their initials) and last name and their mailing address. In addition to introducing you and your company, this less formal, more personal note acknowledges and congratulates their achievement, and it opens the door for a potential discussion with them about finding a new home or for referrals.

<Name of person in the news>,

Congratulations on being named (honored, recognized) as <position, achievement, accomplishment, promotion, award, honor, or designation>.

Although we have never met, I hope you will accept my sincere best wishes on this honor (achievement).

If you think that you might be looking for a new home in the near future, I would enjoy talking with you about it.

Feel free to contact me at <phone number> or <email>. You can learn more about us at <website address>.

All of us here at <name of your company> join in applauding (celebrating) your accomplishment (award, achievement, honor).

Handwritten Greeting Card Note
To People In The News

Use this handwritten note that you create in the blank space above the fold or on the left side of the fold on a commercial greeting card to contact someone proactively because of an article about them you saw online or in your local newspaper — or possibly heard on TV. Only do this if you know their complete first (not just their initials) and last name of the honoree and can get a mailing address for them. Don't write your note over the printed message on the card since you are not a friend and that is a more personal way of writing a message. Besides introducing you and your company, your note acknowledges and congratulates them for their achievement. The rest of your message about wanting to meet them and discuss their housing needs should be saved for later. Your note in this format should be very brief.

———

<Name of person in the news>,

Congratulations on being named (honored) as <position, achievement>. This is quite an opportunity (honor) and one for which you can be proud.

We have never met, but I hope you will accept my sincere best wishes on this honor (achievement). [If you or a family member have received such an award or recognition as well, you can mention it.]

All of us here at <name of your company> join in applauding (celebrating) your accomplishment (award). I look forward to reading more news about you in the future.

Letter To Newlyweds Or Engaged Couples

Use this letter to contact a couple engaged to be married or recently married because of an article about them in your local newspaper. Only do this if you know the names of both the bride and groom and have a mailing address for them. Address your letter to both of them. Besides introducing you and your company, your letter congratulates them on their good news, and it opens the discussion with them about purchasing their first home together.

———

Dear <name of newlyweds or soon-to-be>,

Congratulations on your recent (upcoming) wedding. I saw the announcement in the paper (<name of paper>) on <date of article> (Saturday, recently).

Although we have never met, I want to extend my sincere best wishes for a long and happy life together.

If you are going to be looking for a new home in the

near future or are not certain if you should own a home or rent, I would love to talk with you about your plans and discuss your options.

I can be reached at <phone number> or <email>, and you can learn more about us at <website address>.

All of us here at <name of your company> join in wishing you the very best.

Handwritten Note Or Greeting Card
To Newlyweds Or Engaged Couples

Use this handwritten note or commercial greeting card to contact a couple engaged or recently married from an article about them you saw in your local paper. Only do this if you know the names of both the bride and groom and have a mailing address for them. Address your note or message to both of them. Besides introducing you and your company, your informal, personal note congratulates them on their good news, and it opens the discussion with them about purchasing their first home together.

———

<Name of newlyweds or soon-to-be>,

Congratulations on your recent (upcoming) wedding. I saw the article in the paper (name of paper) on <date of article> (Saturday, over the weekend).

Although we have never met, I want to extend my sincere best wishes for a long and happy life together.

If you are going to be looking for a new home in the near future or are not certain if you should own a home or rent, I would love to talk with you about your plans and discuss your options.

I know that you've got a lot on your minds right now, but feel free to contact me at <phone number> or <email> at your convenience. You can learn more about who we on our website <website address>.

All of us here at <name of your company> join in wishing you the very best.

Letter to Parents — Engagement
Or Wedding Announcement

Use this letter to contact the parent or parents of a son or daughter engaged or getting married that you saw in an article in your local paper. Only do this if you can get the names of one or both of the parents and the son or daughter plus a mailing address for them. Besides introducing you and your company, your letter congratulates them and opens the door for a potential discussion with them about looking for or finding a new home for themselves as well as the soon-to-be newlyweds.

Dear <name of proud parent or parents>,

Congratulations on the upcoming wedding of your son (daughter). I saw the announcement (article) in the paper (<name of paper>) on <date of article> (over the weekend).

Although we have never met, I am happy for you.

If you think you might like a smaller home or one with less maintenance, I would love to discuss what is available for you to consider.

I can be reached at <phone number> or <email>. You can learn more about us at <website address>.

All of us here at <name of your company> join in extending our sincere best wishes to you and your family.

Letter To Parents Of New College Student

Use this letter to contact the parent or parents of a new college student because of an article you saw in your local paper. Only do this if you know one or both of their names and the student's name plus the mailing address for them. Besides introducing you and your company, your letter acknowledges their positive news, and it opens the door for a potential discussion with them about buying a new home.

———

Dear <name of proud parent or parents>,

Congratulations. I just read that your son (daughter) will be attending <name of college or university>. You must be very proud of him/her, and understandably so.

Although we have never met, I am very happy for all of you.

If you are contemplating moving into a smaller home or one with less maintenance in the near future, I would love to discuss what is available for you to consider.

I can be reached at <phone number> or <email>. You also can learn more about us at <website address>.

All of us here at <your company> join in extending our sincere best wishes to you and your family.

Letter To Parents Of College Graduate

Use this letter to contact the parent or parents of a college graduate because of an article about them or their child in your local paper. Only do this if you know one or both of the parents' names and the student's name plus the mailing address for them. Besides introducing you and your company, your letter congratulates them on this accomplishment and opens the door for a potential discussion about buying a new home — them or their son or daughter.

Dear <name of proud parent or parents>,

Congratulations on your son's (daughter's) recent (upcoming) graduation from <name of university>. You must be extremely proud of his/her accomplishment, and understandably so.

Although we have never met, I want to be among the list of well-wishers celebrating your son's/daughter's success.

If you are thinking of moving into a smaller home or one with less maintenance, or if your son/daughter is considering their first home, I would love the opportunity to discuss the opportunities available.

I can be reached at <phone number> or <email>. You can learn more about us at <website address>.

All of us here at <name of your company> join in extending our sincere best wishes on your son's (daughter's) achievement.

Letter Congratulating College Graduate

Use this letter to contact someone because of an article about them graduating from college that you saw in your local paper. Only do this if you know their name and can get a mailing address for them. Besides introducing you and your company, your letter acknowledges their accomplishment, congratulates them on their achievement, and it opens the door for a potential discussion with them about helping them look for a home if they are remaining in your area.

———

Dear <name of recent/soon-to-be graduate>,

Congratulations on your recent (upcoming) graduation. You must be pleased with your accomplishment, as are we.

Although we have never met, I want to be among the list of well-wishers who are celebrating your success.

[If they are staying in the area] As you look for a new residence (place to live), you may be thinking of buying a home. If you're not sure if you should rent or own, I would love the opportunity to discuss your options with you and possibly help you select something.

I can be reached at <phone number> or <email>. You can learn more about us and our homes at <website address>.

All of us here at <your company> join in extending our sincere best wishes on your achievement.

Handwritten Greeting Card Note
To College Graduate

Create a handwritten note in the blank space above the

fold or on the left side of the fold on a commercial greeting card to contact someone because of an article about them graduating from college that you saw online or in your local newspaper. Only do this if you know their complete name and can get a mailing address for them. Don't write over the printed message with your note since you are not a friend and that is a more personal way of writing a message. Besides introducing you and your company, your note acknowledges their achievement and congratulates them on their accomplishment. You are implying that you want to meet them and talk with them about real estate, but this part of your message about meeting them and discussing their housing needs should be saved for later. Your note should be very brief.

———

<Name of college graduate>,

Congratulations on your recent (upcoming) graduation.

This is quite an achievement and one for which you can be very proud.

[If you or a family member (or more than one of you) also graduated from that same school, you can mention it.]

We have never met, but I hope you will accept my sincere best wishes on this accomplishment.

I look forward to reading more about your accomplishments in the years to come.

Letter About Birth Announcement

Use this letter to contact the parents of a new baby because of an article about them you saw in your local newspaper. Only do this if you know their names and can get a mailing address for them. Besides introducing you and your company, your letter congratulates them, and it opens the door for a potential discussion with them about buying a new home and for referrals.

_____

Dear <name or names of new parents>,

Congratulations on the birth of your son (daughter). I saw the announcement (article) in the paper (<name of paper>) on <date of article> (a few days ago, today, yesterday).

Although we have never met, I would like to be among the list of well-wishers for you on this happy (joyous) occasion.

If you think you might need a larger home in the near future or if you have never owned a home of your own before, I would love to talk to you about what we have here at <name of your company>.

I can be reached at <phone number> or <email>.

When you have time, you can learn more about us at <website address>.

All of us at <name of your company> join in celebrating your good news.

Again, best wishes to all of you.

Handwritten Note Or Greeting Card About Birth Announcement

Use this to create a handwritten note on the inside blank page of the commercial greeting card or insert your own note to contact new parents because of a news article about them having a baby that you saw in your local paper. Only do this if you know their names (preferably both parents) and can get a mailing address for them. In addition to introducing you and your company, it congratulates them in a more personal, informal way and opens the door for a potential discussion with them about buying a new home. This is not the time for a strong sales message — just sincere congratulations. Save other messages for later.

———

<Name or names of new parents>,

Congratulations on the birth of your son (daughter)

<son or daughter's name>. I saw the announcement (article) in the paper (<name of paper>) on <date of article> (today, a few days ago, over the weekend).

Although we have never met, I would like to be among the list of well-wishers for you on this happy occasion.

After things settle down a little, I would love to talk to you about the many opportunities available if you think you might need to get a larger home or if you have never owned a home of your own before.

I can be reached at <phone number> or <email>. You can learn more about who we are at <website address>.

Letter To Someone Transferring Or Relocating To Your Area

Use this printed letter to contact someone who is relocating or transferring into your area. Only do this if you learn their complete name and can get a mailing address for them. Besides introducing you and your company, your letter congratulates them on their promotion, transfer, or new position, and it opens the door for a potential discussion with them about helping them buy a new home.

———

Dear <name of transferee>,

Congratulations on your promotion (transfer, relocation). I understand that you are going to be relocating (moving) to <your city or area>, and I want to be one of the first to welcome you to our area.

I know that you are looking forward to coming to a new area but that moving to a new area also presents some challenges, such as finding a new home and locating important services such as dentists, doctors, and schools [if applicable].

I look forward to welcoming you to our area and talking with you about what is available for you to see.

I will call you in a few days to determine what information you would like to receive.

In the meantime, I can be reached at <phone number> or <email>. You can learn more about us at <website address>.

Once again, welcome to <name of city or area>.

I look forward to meeting you when you visit <name of city or area> or officially move to our area.

Letter To HR Department Of Expanding Local Company

Use this letter to contact the human resources

department (HR) of a local company that you are aware of that has announced plans to expand because of an article about their company you saw online or in your local newspaper — or even news that you heard on TV. Besides introducing you and your company, your letter congratulates them for that progress and their success, and it opens the door for a potential discussion with them about working with their employees and helping them select a new home.

———

Dear <name of company official>,

As a fellow corporate citizen of <name of your city or area>, allow us to introduce ourselves to you. We are <name of your company>, and I am <your name>.

[Include a brief paragraph about your market area — which should be within an easy commuting distance to their location or a very desirable area that people want to live in regardless of the commuting distance, and the types of homes or price ranges that you concentrate on to give them a frame of reference. It should line up with what their employees or executives — or both — can afford.]

I have had the pleasure of working with some of your employees already [if this is true], *and I welcome being able to help people that you are bringing into the area find a new home and acclimate to our great city* [if people are coming into the area].

I will call you in a few days to discuss a time when we can meet so I can learn more about your expansion plans and how I can best help you.

In the meantime, I can be reached at <phone number> or <email>. You can learn more about us at <website address>.

Letter To HR Department Of Relocating Non-Local Firm

Use this letter to contact the human resources (HR) department or relocation department of a firm from outside your area that has announced plans to relocate to your market. You may have seen this online or in your local newspaper or even heard it on TV. You may have heard about it through some of your other sources. Besides introducing you and your company, your letter congratulates them on their move, welcomes them to your area, and opens the door for a potential discussion with them about helping their employees find new homes.

———

Dear <name of company official>,

Congratulations on your decision to move your company to (begin operations in, open a division in)

<name of your area>. Let me be among the first to welcome you to our area.

I know that moving to a new area presents a lot of exciting opportunities for your employees, but also presents some challenges, such as finding new homes and locating important services such as dentists, doctors, and schools.

We, like you, are enthusiastic about serving the needs of people in the <name of your city> area.

I look forward to helping people that you are bringing into the area find a new home, and I will call you in a few days to discuss how we can work together.

In the meantime, I can be reached at <phone number> or <email>. You can learn more about us at <website address>.

Once again, welcome to <name of your city or area>. I look forward to meeting you in-person and being able to serve the housing needs of you and your company.

Letter Of Introduction To A Specific Businessperson

Use this letter to contact someone because you know who they are — possibly you are even members of the same organization — but you have never met them.

This letter states what the two of you have in common (if you do) and serves as an introduction of you and your company. It opens the door for a potential discussion with them about their housing needs as well as for those of people they can refer to you. This is the preliminary step to contacting them by phone. Only do this if you know their name and can get a mailing address for them.

———

Dear <name of businessperson>,

Please allow me to introduce myself. We have never formally met, but I have seen you at the <mention the event, group, or location where you have seen them or know of them even if you have not directly seen each other in the past or exchanged a "hello" — such as a luncheon, seminar, fundraiser, large committee meeting, chamber of commerce, church, or civic group>, and I would like to meet you.

I look forward to meeting with you and learning more about your business. I'd also like to talk to you about what I do.

I will give you a call in a couple of days to see when you are available to meet with me for a cup of coffee.

In the meantime, I can be reached at <phone number>

or <email>. You can learn more about us at <website address>.

Letter To Area Businesses
And Professionals

Use this letter to contact area business owners and professionals to introduce you and your company and open the door for a potential discussion with them about their own interest in looking for a new home or people they know who may have an interest in a new home. You are going to be calling them after sending this letter of introduction. This is the first step in meeting them and developing a relationship. Only send this letter if you know their name and can get a mailing address for them.

———

Dear <first name of businessperson, if appropriate>,

I am <your name> of <name of your company> and I'm sending you this brief note to introduce myself and my company. We are your neighbors at <street address or local landmark> [if you are located reasonably close to them — otherwise omit or rephrase this reference].

I'll get right to the point. I can use your help.

Like you, we are quite excited about serving the needs of people in the <name of your city> area.

I will call you in a few days to see if (when) we can schedule a time for a cup of coffee so I can learn a little more about your business and share with you what I have in mind.

In the meantime, I can be reached at <phone number> or <email>. You can learn more about us at <website address>.

Letter To A Nearby Renter

Use this letter to contact residents of a nearby rental complex about the possibilities of home ownership. Only do this if you can get their name and a mailing address for them. Do not use a generic greeting like "Dear Neighbor," "Dear Renter," or "Our Friends At" because that has the characteristics of a direct mailing piece. Your letter will introduce you and your company and open the door for a potential discussion with them about buying a new home.

———

Dear <name or names of renter or renters>,

Allow me to introduce myself. I am <your name> of <name of your company>, your neighbor at <address, local landmark, or point of reference>.

I am contacting you because I want to talk with you about owning your own home that I can help you find.

We have many wonderful financing plans available also [if this is true].

I can be reached at <phone number> or <email>. You can learn more about us at <website address>.

If you like, just drop into our office and ask for me. Our hours are <state hours>.

Letter To An Area Homeowner

Use this letter to contact someone because they live in your general market area — do not send this if their home is listed with another Realtor® as evidenced by a yard sign or MLS record. Your letter introduces you and your company, and it opens the door for a potential discussion with them about putting their current home on the market and looking for a new home. Only do this if you can get their name and a mailing address for them. Otherwise, it does not have the same impact or connection.

─────

Dear <name or names of owner or owners>,

Allow me to introduce myself. I am <your name> of <name of your company>, your neighbor at <address, local landmark, or point of reference>.

If you have been (are) thinking of (thinking about,

considering, talking about) selling your present home and looking for something else, I'd like to talk with you to help you evaluate the value of your current home and find out what you might be looking for in another one.

Plus, we have many wonderful financing plans (incentives) available [if this is true].

Regardless of whether you are currently looking for a new home or plan on doing so in the near future, I'd still like to meet you or talk with you.

Letter To A New Area Resident

Use this letter to contact someone because you have learned that they recently moved into your general market area. Your letter introduces you and your company, and it opens the door for a potential discussion with them about referrals and looking for a new home in the future. Only do this if you can get their name and a mailing address for them.

———

Dear <name of new area resident>,

Welcome to the neighborhood!

Allow us to introduce ourselves. I am <your name> of <name of your company>, your neighbor at <actual

address, landmark, or point of reference>.

We wish you all the best as you settle in to this area and would love to have you stop by for a "neighborly" cup of coffee at your convenience. Our hours are <state hours>.

If I can help you in any way — such as helping you locate any services or facilities — please call me at <telephone number> or email me at <address>. You also may visit us at <website address> to learn more about who we are.

I look forward to meeting you.

Letter To A "FSBO"

Use this letter to contact a homeowner in your market area that has a "For Sale By Owner" sign in their yard. **Assure them that you are not trying to list their home for them** — because they likely have had several Realtors® already approach them. You want to introduce yourself, find out about the interest they've had in their home, talk with them about selecting their next home from you if they haven't made a decision on one yet, and learn who else they know who might be interested in buying a new home.

———

Dear <name of seller>,

I saw your "For Sale" sign as I was driving by today (I saw your home for sale in <name of publication>), but I am not contacting you about helping you to sell your current home.

Rather, I would appreciate the opportunity of meeting (talking) with you about your options for your next home if you have not already made a decision on it.

I can be reached at <phone number> or <email>. You can learn more about who we are at <website address>.

Feel free to call me just to ask a question at <telephone number>. I'll help out any way that I can.

Good luck on the sale of your home!

7

Making It Work

An Entrepreneurial Approach

As an entrepreneur, you have no customers. They don't come in the box you get when you decide to go into business.

You're starting from scratch. You examine your options for customers — the lifeblood of your business — and determine that you have three viable choices.

Option one — you stay in your office or open house and greet the people or sales leads that contact you through conventional means. This includes all forms of print advertising, signage, electronic media, internet, other broker traffic, and incidental referrals.

Of course, you maintain post-visit Follow-Through® contact with everyone you meet according to their level of interest and ability to make a decision.

Option two — you talk to people you already know and begin developing your own leads. This is discussed in my companion book for lead generation: *"Utilizing Your Contacts: More Realty Listings & Sales With People You Already Know."*

Option three — you reach out to people you don't know or haven't met. You involve strangers in your business and begin building sales and referrals with their help.

This is what we've been discussing and preparing you for in this book, and this is where you have the greatest freedom and potential to make it really big.

This is what's going to give you the additional edge and earning power over other real estate professionals in your market.

Most Realtors® are content to work with the people that contact them from various sources (including other Realtors®) or incidental referrals.

This is unpredictable and shortsighted. It is not a dependable or consistent form of lead generation.

Empowering Yourself For Success

With the knowledge that you can produce your own leads and make traffic appear that you have generated, you can be an outstanding success.

This is powerful.

By reaching out to people that you don't know, you're going to be adding an element to your sales program that most Realtors® and real estate sales professionals are missing.

There is no effective limit to the number of leads that you can generate this way. You have the power to be as successful as you want.

Generating your own leads — particularly by reaching out to meet, contact, and begin working with people you don't know — can make the difference in your success. It will enable you to make a bold statement about how you view your business and allow you to thrive in your marketplace.

You will be eliminating the total dependence on your broker or company and conventional marketing and advertising as the source of your contacts and leads.

Empowerment Is Taken

Empowering yourself to begin generating your own leads — by working with either friends or strangers — is not something you have to be invited to do or given permission to start.

Empowerment is taken. It is not given.

Just decide that generating your own leads is something that makes sense for you to do — even if you're not totally comfortable with the idea of meeting strangers and developing them into sales leads or referrals.

Then, you will have empowered yourself to begin expanding your business and taking responsibility for producing the most crucial element of your sales program — your future customers.

Going Beyond The Obvious

While talking to people that you already know and asking them for referrals will net you many additional opportunities to make sales (and I certainly recommend that you do this), other ambitious real estate professionals can do the same thing within their circle or sphere of contacts.

They may not be as comprehensive as you are or able to identify the variety of people that you can contact, but starting with referrals from existing satisfied customers and from family and friends are common ways to generate more potential business.

Add to that, the other broker activity that many Realtors® try to attract for selling their listings, and you'll soon see that this is a very competitive way of attracting new business.

Nevertheless, when you use some of the scenarios and strategies that are in my companion lead generation book, *"Utilizing Your Contacts: More Realty Listings & Sales With People You Already Know,"* you'll be doing considerably more than the average Realtor® or real estate sales professional and definitely going beyond the obvious.

However, to really gain the advantage in your marketplace, begin using the techniques for meeting and working with strangers that I've given you in these pages here. Few other Realtors® and real estate sales professionals in your market will come close to the type of lead generation you'll be capable of producing.

Reaching out to total strangers and strategically contacting other businesspeople and professionals in your marketplace that can help you in your business are ways that you can be intentional and proactive about expanding your business.

Intentionally Going After Success

Making the decision that you want to have more contacts and sales leads than you're getting now through traditional or conventional sources — and that you want it on a more consistent basis — is the first step to becoming a great lead generator.

It is a conscious decision, and it requires willpower and

commitment — as well as the ability to persevere and remain with it.

No one reaches this intentional decision without the earnest desire to act on it — unless it is just wishful thinking.

Wanting more contacts — as in it sure would be nice to have — is entirely different than doing something to actually make it happen.

This works in all market conditions — very competitive markets to very stubborn ones.

As long as there are homes to sell and people to buy them, the techniques and strategies of lead generation that I've discussed will work for you.

What better way to really go after potential customers than to begin meeting people that are not currently part of your circle or sphere of contacts?

The Power Of Strangers

The reason I've created this book for you that focuses on attracting and working with strangers is that they are limitless.

We are always meeting new people. We can intentionally insert ourselves into a situation where there will be new people around us for us to make the initial contact. We just have to be where there is an opportunity to meet and engage people that we may not already know.

If we stay in our offices all day, go straight home when we leave the office, and hang around the house most of the time when we aren't at the office, we are going to have very limited opportunities to meet additional people.

Working with people we already know is great — that's an important component of generating our own leads. However, working with strangers is a concept few salespeople ever grasp.

You're In Charge Now

The amount of traffic you can produce is limited only by your ambition and the amount of time devoted to it.

You have been given several scenarios and strategies in this book. Expand from there. This is a good start, but it is not intended to be exhaustive.

Begin thinking of even more ways that you can be around people that you may not know so that you can say hello to them and begin developing the contact.

Not every casual contact will develop into a sales lead

or referral.

Some people will stop you at just the initial contact, but others will allow you to call them.

Act as if the only traffic you're going to get is what you produce for yourself.

This is the real key to your success.

You have to own your customer base — go after it, produce it, and be responsible for it. You have to continually add to it so it doesn't get stale. Own the creation of additional leads.

Your paradigm needs to be that you're in charge of producing the people that you will talk with to create listings and make sales.

Anything else that comes your way through traditional or conventional advertising and marketing produced by your company or broker, and incidental referrals from people you've already met in your office or open houses, will just be a bonus.

Steve Hoffacker

Steve Hoffacker, AICP, CAASH, CAPS, CGA, CGP, CMP, CSP, MCSP, MIRM, is principal of Hoffacker Associates LLC, a West Palm Beach, Florida based real estate and new home sales training company, marketing consultancy and commercial real estate brokerage.

Steve is an award-winning new home sales trainer, real estate sales coach, marketing consultant, award-winning photographer, commercial real estate broker, blogger, and best-selling author of instructional sales books.

For more than 30 years, he has helped homebuilders, new home salespeople, contractors, Realtors® and real estate sales professionals, small business owners, and entrepreneurs to be more visible, competitive, profitable, and effective — and to really enjoy what they are doing.

One of the keys to increased production and profitability is Steve's innovative customer connection program of intentional lead generation, customer rating, social networking, and post-visit contact that lets you reach out to potential customers, attract new leads, identify those people who are ready to make a decision, and maintain appropriate contact with others who need more time.

As a result, you will be making sales that otherwise might not have happened, and you can eliminate unnecessary expenditures of time, money, and energy in the process.

www.ingramcontent.com/pod-product-compliance
Lightning Source LLC
Chambersburg PA
CBHW061217220326
41599CB00025B/4669